Everyday Consciousness and Buddha-Awakening

Everyday Consciousness and Buddha-Awakening

Khenchen Thrangu Rinpoche

Translated and edited by Susanne Schefczyk

Snow Lion Publications
Ithaca, New York
Boulder, Colorado

Snow Lion Publications
P.O. Box 6483
Ithaca, New York 14851 USA
607-273-8519
www.snowlionpub.com

Printed in Canada on acid-free, recycled paper.

ISBN 1-55939-170-7

Library of Congress Cataloging-in-Publication Data
Thrangu, Rinpoche, 1933-
  Everyday consciousness and Buddha-awakening / Khenchen Thrangu Rinpoche ; translated and edited by Susanne Schefczyk.
    p. cm.
Includes bibliographical references.
  ISBN 1-55939-170-7
  1. Meditation--Buddhism. 2. Consciousness--Religious aspects--Buddhism. 3. Buddhism--Doctrines. I. Schefczyk, Susanne, 1959– II. Title.
  BQ5612 .T5 2002
  294.3'444--dc21
                                          2001007264

CONTENTS

Translator's Preface

Thrangu Rinpoche is one of the most learned masters of the Karma Kagyü lineage of Tibetan Buddhism. He holds the title of 'Khenchen' (Great Scholar), because after fleeing from Tibet to India, it was he who taught Tibetan philosophy to the four lineage-holders and it was he who for many years was the main abbot of the monastic university in exile at Rumtek, Sikkim, in India. Thus he was responsible for the education of most of the present-day scholars of this lineage. At present, being the main teacher of H.H. the Seventeenth Karmapa, Urgyen Thrinley Dorje, Thrangu Rinpoche plays an important role in preserving the unbroken continuation of the Karma Kagyü lineage.

Rinpoche not only shares his knowledge with disciples from the East, but for more than twenty years now has regularly travelled to the West in order to introduce Tibetan philosophy to those educated in Western school-systems.

In July 1997, he visited the Kamalashila Institute for Buddhist Studies in Germany to introduce Buddhist psychology to his German disciples according to Mipham Rinpoche's *Gateway to Knowledge* (Tib. *mKhas 'jug*). A year later, in August 1998, he visited the retreat center in Halscheid to teach on *The Commentary that Distinguishes Consciousness from Primordial Awareness* (Tib. *rNam shes ye shes 'byed pa'i bstan bcos*), a treatise by the Third Karmapa, Rangjung Dorje.

On both these opportunities I served as his interpreter, and, though I had studied and translated these same topics several times before, I was impressed by the detailed yet very clear and comprehensible presentation with which Rinpoche described the functions of mind, perception, and consciousnesses in contrast to buddha-awareness, which in the West are an uncommon form of knowledge. Thrangu Rinpoche fuses philosophy with precise meditation instructions in such a way as to enable the participants to understand and reflect on their own state and function of the consciousnesses as he was teaching, and thereby to enhance their development of the primordial buddha-awarenesses. I felt that these teachings should be made available to a broader audience in the West, and so I proposed to Rinpoche that I make a book of these two series of talks. Rinpoche happily agreed.

For this book I retranslated and transcribed the talks afresh from the tapes, my intention being to remain as faithful as possible to what Rinpoche originally said. This also facilitated the removal of vaguenesses and misinterpretations in my original oral translation. It is extremely important to translate as precisely as possible the process of perception according to Buddhist psychology. Many Tibetan words have no precise correlates in Western terminology; moreover, if Western psychological terms were to be used to interpret Buddhist thought, this could easily lead to a wrong understanding of what was actually said. This is also why, at the end of the book, I include a detailed glossary of the Tibetan terminology and my corresponding translation. In this way the well-versed reader is able to recognize the original term of the translation, and translators may use this to discuss or further develop the English terms.

Fusing these two series of talks, I have thus presented Mipham's explanation of the consciousnesses and their transformation into primordial awareness. In a few instances this differs from what Rangjung Dorje says; these differences are listed in the end-notes. The meditation based on the consciousnesses and the meditation to develop primordial awareness were taken in toto from Thrangu Rinpoche's second series of talks. Since the audience of these talks was German, and the participants were awaiting a transcript to study the teachings more thoroughly, this book was published initially in German as *Alltagsbewußtsein & Buddha-Erwachen*. Thanks to the inspired interest of Sidney Piburn and Jeff Cox from Snow Lion Publications, it is now possible to make these talks available to an English-speaking public as well. The English book further includes explanations on the transformation of the five elements into the five female Buddhas which Thrangu Rinpoche taught in August 1998 in Freiburg and which were not available at the time of the German publication.

The language for technical Buddhism is much more developed in English than in German, and therefore it is generally easier to translate such talks into English. However, the main difficulty in translating the Buddhist science of cognition lies in the different views of the different Buddhist schools of thought. These are principally divided into, first, the Hinayana schools of the Vaibashikas and Sautrantikas, and, second, the Mahayana schools of the Chittamatrins and the Madhyamikas. All of them, however, use the relatively clear and easily understandable presentation of mind and perception of the Sautrantika philosophy, Sautrantika terminology included. Nevertheless, what in the end is accepted as valid cognition by the different schools of thought varies quite considerably.

For example, when Rinpoche says: "The consciousness leaves through the gate of the eye to be able to perceive outer form ..." (page 22), at once the question arises—how is it possible that the consciousness, which is mind, can come into contact with a sense object, which is matter? This is not a question for us alone, for this was one of the problems that sparked off the differing views on the absolute truth of the different philosophical schools of Buddhism. It is only from the point of view of the Vaibashika school that consciousness, sense faculty, and sense object can actually make contact, and thereby the mind perceive its object. According to the view of the Sautrantikas, the outer reality cannot be directly perceived at all. They say therefore that the objects leave an image of themselves in the mind so that this mental image may be perceived by the mental consciousness. Due to this postulation the followers of the Chittamatra school came to doubt the existence of the outer reality, even considering it unnecessary. Why? Because mind just perceives mind anyway! From the mental consciousness merely perceiving mental images they conclude that everything—that is, the outer reality as well as the inner mind—is merely mind only. The conclusion of the views of the Madhyamaka schools goes even one step further still. They ask themselves, If the outer perceived objects do not exist truly and independently, then how could a perceiver of these objects exist in such a way? If nothing real is to be perceived, how can a perceiver that is based on something to be perceived come about? This means that, from the point of view of the Madhyamikas, ultimately the perceiving mind itself—that is, the consciousness—cannot truly exist either.

The Buddhist scholars teaching about mind still use the terminology of the Sautrantikas even if their own ultimate view differs, since it is quite readily understandable by ordinary people. They see no problem using it, because the ultimate view is always vivid in their minds. If we, however, discover contradictions in their talks, this is just because we Western students were educated to doubt and to criticize. Thus we must learn to distinguish between the conventional terminology and what is meant by it from the ultimate view of the individual philosophical school of thought. For example, in this present book Thrangu Rinpoche speaks of the 'attainment of primordial awareness' several times, but actually primordial awareness is not to be 'attained' nor to be 'developed'. From the point of view of the Yogachara-madhyamaka school (Shentong), primordial awareness is what is fully present from the very beginning and what merely has to be laid bare by removing delusion. Thrangu Rinpoche reveals the methods to do so in this book.

It was only thanks to close cooperation with Karl Brunnhölzl that it was possible for me to publish this book in a precise translation. As a physician, a translator of Tibetan, and an expert in Pramana (the Buddhist science of cognition and psychology), he is informed about the physical processes of perception and in addition qualified to judge my translation. I am extremely grateful to him for examining both the German and the English manuscripts for any errors in logic, and for helping to clarify several philosophical points I had inadvertently overlooked. For their help in clarifying specific details in connection with the sense faculties, I wish to thank Elizabeth Callahan, expert in Vajrayana terminology, and Daniel Winkler, expert in Tibetan botanical science. And it was Acharya Lama Tenpa Gyaltsen who always found the solution to what initially appeared to be intractable problems in philosophy and language.

Once the talks were translated and all preliminary problems sorted out, the book was not as readable as it could be. The manuscript needed to be screened several times by someone conversant with the topic who in addition had native English skills. I thank Lee Bray for his contribution in this regard, although the final choice of technical terminology remains mine. Furthermore, I wish to thank Manuela Rasquin-Wirth for all her loving support, and all my dharma friends, including my family, for their unceasing encouragement that allows me to continue my translating work.

I am positive that the knowledge Thrangu Rinpoche shares with us in this book will help dharma practitioners to realize the aims of their practice. So I wish that through the merit created by everyone in the evolution of this book, all sentient beings may actualize primordial awareness and become Buddhas.

Susanne Schefczyk
Lensahnerhof, May 2001

Introduction by Thrangu Rinpoche

I am particularly happy to have the opportunity here to explain the difference between everyday consciousness and the primordial awareness of the Buddhas. In my opinion, knowledge about the mind is very beneficial for everyone. Mind is designated as being composed of six, or sometimes eight, collections of consciousness. This is a very specific classification of mind as generally taught in Buddhist philosophy, but one which is comprehensible by means of inference.

Everyone who meditates—including those who, for example, are visualizing the creation phase of a yidam deity—will receive much greater benefit from the meditation if they know about the condition of mind. Whoever meditates on calm abiding (Skt. *shamatha*) should, while doing so, be clear about what 'the resting mind' actually is, and how it may be generated. For the meditation on deep insight (Skt. *vipashyana*) of the great seal (Skt. *mahamudra*) or of the great perfection (Skt. *mahasandi*), it is likewise of great benefit to know what the mind is composed of, what its innate essence is, and through which forms of expression it makes itself manifest.

Studying this topic is also beneficial for those who are interested in Western psychology and psychotherapy. Some psychologists conscientiously study the mind's mode of being according to the teachings of Buddhism. They are very much interested in the divisions of mind into six or eight kinds of consciousness, and how these consciousnesses function.

Knowledge about the five kinds of primordial awareness is also important, since this is the fruit that all practicing Buddhists aspire to bring forth through their meditation and dharma practice. The fruit of this practice is to reveal the ultimate primordial awareness. Since meditation takes us gradually closer to this result, it is important to know about what results may be attained.

Though the highest, ultimate result of our dharma practice is the state of a Buddha, this does not mean that we leave off being present to ourselves and our situation and pass over to somewhere else entirely. Nor are we to be concerned with developing extraordinary powers to boast about or with which to show off. Instead it is a case of revealing the primordial awareness that is primordially present within ourselves. It reveals itself through the gradual development of the three kinds of highest understanding (Skt. *prajña*): that arisen through listening, that arisen through reflecting, and that arisen through meditating. When these three are completely and perfectly developed, the primordial awareness is fully revealed.

Due to the influence of primordial awareness expanding, the stains of ignorance and obscuration become purified, and we attain the ultimate fruit that in Sanskrit is called 'Buddha'. The Tibetan equivalent of this designation is 'sang-gye' (Tib. *sangs rgyas*), 'purified and expanded'. The actual meaning of 'Buddha' is merely 'gye', 'expanded'. The Tibetan translators, however, added the syllable 'sang', 'purified', in order to indicate that due to primordial awareness revealing itself all the obscurations are purified. Thus in Tibetan the designation 'Buddha' in both its aspects, that of purification and that of expansion, points to primordial awareness.

The method to expand the primordial awareness consists principally of engaging in meditation. Therefore, in order to practice and meditate correctly, we should first of all understand what primordial awareness is and how it reveals itself. This knowledge can be attained through the highest understanding of listening and reflecting.

When Buddha Shakyamuni introduced the Buddhist teachings (Skt. *dharma*) he taught extensively on the subject of the mind. In the context of the lesser vehicle (Skt. *hinayana*), when explaining the five aggregates, the twelve sense-sources, and the eighteen elements,[1] the Buddha explained the mind in terms of six collections of consciousness: eye, ear, nose, tongue, and body consciousness (i.e., the five sense consciousnesses), and the mind consciousness.

In the context of the great vehicle (Skt. *mahayana*), however, Buddha Shakyamuni explained the mind in terms of the eight collections of consciousness: the seventh consciousness is the klesha-mind and the eighth the all-base consciousness (Skt. *alayavijñana*). The reason why these two types of consciousness were not taught in the lesser vehicle is explained in the sutras. There it says, "the absorbing consciousness[2] is profound and subtle. If it were taken to be the self, that would not be appropriate."[3] The all-base consciousness functions uninterruptedly, like the flow of a river, by absorbing imprints as seeds. In many non-Buddhist philosophies—for example, that of the Indian Tirthikas—the true existence of a self is postulated. It could happen that the followers of such philosophies take the all-base consciousness to be the truly existent self; this is a mistake. In the great vehicle, however, there is no entity as such that could be viewed as the self: indeed, there is no valid cognition that could prove the true existence of such a self. Since sometimes the body is taken to be the self and sometimes also the mind, there is no definite focal point for the self. It obviously follows that the self cannot be construed as being the all-base consciousness either.

When the Buddha's teaching spread throughout India, many Indian scholars (Skt. *pandita*) wrote commentaries. When Buddhism later came to Tibet, Tibetan scholars also wrote commentaries concerning the functioning condition of the mind. Explanations of the most important points describing the functions of mind were given by Karmapa Rangjung Dorje in his text *The Commentary that Distinguishes Consciousness from Primordial Awareness*. In addition, Mipham Rinpoche addressed the same topic in his text *Gateway to Knowledge*.[4] Both these texts describe the functions of the eight kinds of consciousness, the way they can be transformed into the five kinds of primordial awareness, and how the ultimate fruit—the level of the five buddha-families—can be attained.

Concerning the transformation of the eight consciousnesses into the five kinds of primordial awareness, however, the authors each emphasize different aspects. Karmapa Rangjung Dorje emphasizes the seventh consciousness by dividing it into two kinds: the 'immediate mind' and the 'klesha-mind'. Mipham Rinpoche, however, describes the all-base consciousness in much more detail by discriminating between the 'all-base' and the 'all-base consciousness'.

When I was seventeen years old I studied Mipham Rinpoche's text very intensely. At such a young age one learns very well, and this is why I still remember his interpretation very clearly today. The following explanations are therefore in accordance with Mipham Rinpoche's text *Gateway to Knowledge*.

I
EVERYDAY CONSCIOUSNESS

Chapter One

THE SIX COLLECTIONS OF CONSCIOUSNESS

Let's first look at ourselves. Within the realms of sentient beings, we have taken on a human body. A human being consists of body, speech, and mind; these are called the three gates. As for the gate of speech, it is nothing other than the sounds with which we can express ourselves and which can be heard by others. Much more important is our body and our mind. Depending on the circumstances, it is sometimes our body that is the center of our concern, but at other times it is also our mind. Body and mind are closely connected, so that we consider them practically the same, as if they had the same essence. But if we analyze more closely we find that our body is 'matter composed of atoms'[5] and our mind is something that is 'clear and cognizing'.[6] As for the body, there have to be many different components to make up the flesh, the blood, the bones, the intestines, and so forth, so that the whole body is formed. The mind, however, has completely different characteristics. It is not matter, nor is it composed of atoms. Mind is defined as 'clear and cognizing'. It is the mind that knows and understands things. That's how, through detailed analysis, we can come to understand that body and mind are completely different in terms of their essence.

Though body and mind differ from the point of view of their essence, nevertheless we can't separate them. This is

due to the fact that for as long as we live the body is dependent on our mind and, vice versa, the mind is bound to our
body. That's why we see them as a unit. However, we should
absolutely be able to distinguish between these two.
Therefore, we shall analyze mind separately here.

Mind is described as the eight collections of consciousness. Of course, mind in its essence is just one, but it can be
divided by means of eight different aspects of consciousness,
each of which has its distinct characteristics.

As long as sentient beings dwell within conditioned existence, known as the impure phase,[7] mind expresses itself
in the form of the eight collections of consciousness. As a
result of dharma practice and meditative concentration (Skt.
samadhi), the eight kinds of consciousness will be purified.
At that point they will transform and thus reveal themselves
to be the five kinds of primordial awareness. In order to
understand the essence of these five kinds of awareness,
we first have to look at the eight collections of consciousness.

Understanding how consciousness transforms itself into
primordial awareness also helps us to understand the way
the paths to buddhahood are traversed and which kinds of
result can be attained by each path. Furthermore, it contains a temporary benefit for our meditation practice, which
is to know how meditation functions. This is valid for meditation on the body of a deity as well as for other kinds of
meditative concentration, such as calm abiding or deep insight. For those times when we just let our mind rest within
itself, it is very beneficial to know about the characteristics
and divisions of the eight kinds of consciousness.

For the meditation on the nature of your own mind it is
customary to ask your teacher for pointing-out instructions.
Some practitioners are lucky enough to recognize their true
nature of mind straight away, whereas others merely perceive a sensation of it, a certain experience of the true nature
of mind. But if they don't know exactly how mind and the
consciousnesses function, their experience will dissolve after a few days. The understanding of mind and the eight

kinds of consciousness is obtained through the highest understanding (Skt. *prajña*) of listening and reflecting.[8] When we really meditate on this basis and glimpse the true nature of mind, we will be able to steadily increase our experience of it through all subsequent meditation. That's why it is extremely useful to know about the eight kinds of consciousness.

A beginner who visualizes the body of a deity and does not know the distinctive characteristics of the different aspects of consciousness would think that the deity must be seen as clearly during the mental meditation as if seen directly with the eyes. The eyes, however, have a much coarser way of perceiving concrete forms. Beginners do indeed meditate in the hope of attaining such clarity. Nevertheless, it will not arise, because the meditation on a deity does not happen through the medium of the eye consciousness, but through the medium of the mind consciousness. The objects of the mind consciousness are much less clear. The mind consciousness most definitely does not work like the eye consciousness. That's why some meditators who perceive a vague mental image think they are not capable of meditating correctly on a deity. The result is that they develop an aversion for their meditation. Those, however, who understand that each consciousness perceives in a different way know that mental images aren't as clear as the forms perceived with the eyes, and therefore they are content with their meditation. They know how to meditate, do indeed so meditate, and thus their meditation works well.

THE FIVE SENSE CONSCIOUSNESSES

The consciousnesses are divided into two categories: 'stable consciousnesses' and 'unstable consciousnesses'. An unstable consciousness arises and vanishes straight away. After that, a new unstable consciousness arises which also vanishes straight away. A stable consciousness, however, lasts all the time. No matter what you are doing, it will not vanish. Nevertheless, it is much easier to recognize an unstable consciousness.

Six kinds of consciousnesses are categorized as unstable consciousnesses. These are the five sense consciousnesses and the mind consciousness. Again these can be divided into 'thought-free' consciousnesses and one consciousness 'involving thoughts'. All of the sense consciousnesses are thought-free, because they merely perceive their specific object without any kind of conceptual associations happening. The mere sense consciousnesses do not make up thoughts such as "That's good" or "That's bad." At the moment of perception there is also no sensation of desire or anger.[9] The mind consciousness, however, takes its form in connection with thoughts of attachment and aversion, thinking "That's good," "That's bad," "What's that?" "I need this," or "I don't want that." Therefore, it is called a consciousness involving thoughts.

In Tibetan the five sense consciousnesses are called the consciousnesses of the five gates. 'Gate' is used here as an example. As with a house—if you want to go outside, you need a door to do so—so it is with each sense consciousness. It leaves through the gate of the eye to be able to perceive outer form, or through the gate of the ear to be able to perceive outer sound. In the same way the different inner consciousnesses leave through the gate of the nose, through the gate of the tongue, or through the gate of the body to clearly perceive an outer object. That's why these consciousnesses are called the consciousnesses of the five gates.

Each of the five kinds of thought-free sense consciousness arises based on a specific sense faculty. First of all, the consciousness that is based on the eye faculty: It perceives visible form as its specific object of perception; that is, anything that arises as outer form. This consciousness is called the 'eye consciousness' and its defining characteristic is 'to see form'. Other than form, there is no sense object that it can perceive. It does not hear sounds, nor does it smell odors, recognize tastes, or sense any physical sensations. Generally this is so with any consciousness: it perceives just its own specific sense object. Thus it is the specific function of the eye consciousness to perceive outer form, and to do so it relies on the inner sense faculty of the eyes. This so-called eye faculty is an extremely subtle faculty within the eyes. As the eyeball is the basis for the eye faculty, it is thus called the 'faculty basis'. The Buddha and all the siddhas who are endowed with extrasensory perception and who are able to work miracles describe the eye faculty thus: the faculty that gives rise to the eye consciousness looks like a flax flower,[10] blue and extremely small and subtle. However, it is no coarse form consisting of atoms, but a 'clear form', a manifestation of light. When a person dies, or when the sense organs are damaged and cease to function, the clear form of the sense faculty dissolves. It won't remain. In a living person, however, it is present as a manifestation within the sense organ. Within the eyes, the eye faculty takes on the form of a flax flower.

The second of the five sense consciousnesses is the ear consciousness. It arises based on the sense faculty of the ears. It cannot view forms, nor can it perceive the other sense objects except for sound, since its specific object of perception is sound. But it can perceive sound of any quality, whether it is loud or low, pleasant or unpleasant. In general, the ear consciousness arises in our ears. Again, however, it is not the ears themselves, but the ear faculty that is within them that gives rise to the consciousness. It is described in the following way: the ear faculty is like the knotty protuberances in the bark of birch trees.[11] Its clear form is also a manifestation of light. Though it is said to be a form, it is not a coarse but an extremely subtle form. When it is damaged, it dissolves without leaving a findable residue. Yet the ear consciousness can only perceive sound on the basis of this subtle light manifestation of the ear faculty.

The third consciousness, the nose consciousness, functions in the same way. It just perceives smells as its specific object, good smells, bad smells, natural smells and also manufactured smells. The perception of smells is based on the nose faculty, the subtle manifestation of light that re-sembles two parallel, extremely fine copper needles.[12] In the sutras the Buddha describes them as copper-colored. Based on this nose faculty, the nose consciousness arises, and smells can be perceived.

The fourth consciousness is the tongue consciousness. It perceives only tastes as its specific object, and it is based on the tongue faculty. This faculty is described by the Buddha in the sutras and also by the siddhas who possess extrasen-sory perception: the sense faculty that gives rise to the tongue consciousness resembles the half-moon.[13] It is found on the tongue as its faculty basis. This light manifestation gives rise to the tongue consciousness so that tastes such as sweet, sour, and so forth can be perceived as the specific sense objects.

The fifth consciousness is the body consciousness. It per-ceives everything physically tangible as its specific object, such as what is soft, hard, or rough. The body conscious-ness also arises based on an inner sense faculty, namely the body faculty. The sense faculties of the first four conscious-nesses are specific faculties that are found in a special loca-tion within the body. The body faculty, however, is not specially bound to one location, but instead spread over the whole body from head to toe, except for the hair and nails. It also permeates the body from the outer skin to the inner organs, including the skeleton. That's why everything tan-gible can be perceived both outwardly at the body surface and inwardly within the interior of the body itself. The body faculty is said to be like the covering skin of the bird 'Soft to Touch',[14] and it takes shape and color according to the part of the body that it covers. At the skin it is skin-colored, and at the bones it is bone-colored. Here, also, the faculty is just a clear manifestation of light.

Without closer examination it seems to us as if we see something with our eyes. Since the eyeballs are the basis for the eye faculty, we consequently think that it is the fac-ulty basis that would perceive form. However, the eye is of material form, a form made of atoms which cannot see in the least.[15] Nevertheless, it is the abode of the eye faculty. Thus the question arises whether it is the eye faculty that perceives the outer forms. The sense faculty, however, cannot see, because it is a material form as well, though only a very subtle material form which gives rise to a consciousness that in its essence is clear and cognizing. It is a knowing with a clear and cognizing appearance. So it is not the eye itself that sees the form, but the eye consciousness. In the same way it is not the ear that hears the sound, but the ear consciousness, because the consciousness has a clear and cognizing appearance. The same is valid for all of the five senses. If we think the sense faculties of the body perceive the sense objects, that's not true. They nevertheless constitute the basis for a consciousness to arise, and due to the arising of the consciousness the sense object is perceived. Thus perception can only function if three factors come together: an object, the corresponding sense faculty, and the corresponding consciousness. If, for instance, the object is a form with shape and color, and if it meets with the eye faculty, an eye consciousness can arise so that this form is perceived.

THE MIND CONSCIOUSNESS

The five sense consciousnesses are the thought-free consciousnesses. They directly perceive the object and cannot create thoughts. The consciousness involving thoughts is the mind consciousness. It is the thinker who entertains all the different thoughts. The mind consciousness does not have a specific gate through which to leave as the sense consciousnesses of the five gates do, because there is no definite location with which it can be associated. The scholars and siddhas of Buddhist philosophy call it 'the sixth, the mind consciousness', because when they expound on the consciousnesses they generally present the five sense consciousnesses first and then, as the sixth, the mind consciousness. Thus when they talk of the sixth consciousness as such, the 'six' has no other meaning than a merely numerical one.

Usually we create many thoughts such as "I am fine" or "I am miserable." In this way as well, positive thoughts of loving-kindness and compassion arise, as also do negative thoughts such as those of anger or desire. When we are extremely happy, of course it is a case of having happy thoughts, and when we are sad, unhappy thoughts arise. All this kind of thinking is called the mind consciousness.

The mind consciousness has different defining characteristics than the above-described five kinds of sense consciousness, each of which is based on a sense faculty, a clear form composed of light. For the mind consciousness this is not the case. It is not based on a clear form, a sense faculty. That raises the question, upon which basis does the mind consciousness arise? It arises immediately after a sense consciousness. Thus a preceding eye, ear, nose, tongue, or body consciousness serves as its basis. In the case that there is no arising of any of the five sense consciousnesses, the mind consciousness can also arise after the preceding moment of a mind consciousness. In that way one mind consciousness arises immediately after the other, and its 'sense' faculty is not a clear form, but consciousness. Thus mind consciousness is based on any preceding moment of consciousness, no matter which kind of the six collections of consciousness it is.

What kind of object does the mind consciousness perceive? The Buddhist scholars call the specific object of perception of the mind consciousness 'phenomena'. Within the sphere of phenomena each kind of sense object can appear as an object of the mind consciousness; thus any form, sound, smell, taste, and physically tangible object can also appear as an object of the mind consciousness, not only all the outer but also all the inner objects.[16] These objects can all appear, but they do not appear directly. The mind consciousness creates an image of the perceived objects, which means the external visual form is not seen by the mind consciousness, but instead a mental image similar to that perceived by the eye consciousness appears to the perspective of the mind consciousness. Or, an appearance similar to the sound that is perceived by the ear consciousness appears to the perspective of the mind consciousness. In the same way, there appear mental images similar to the smells, tastes, or physically tangible objects that are perceived by the remaining sense consciousnesses. This is why the mind consciousness apprehends all of the outer objects, but cannot perceive them clearly.

The mind consciousness does not recognize clearly, does not see clearly, nor does it perceive the sense objects clearly. Nevertheless, it is endowed with extraordinary qualities that are not shared with the sense consciousnesses. Its special qualities are the many different thoughts that appear within it. In this way, among all the six collections of consciousnesses, the mind consciousness has the busiest job! The five sense consciousnesses merely perceive. The mind consciousness, however, judges this mere perception immediately afterwards with thoughts such as "That's good" or "That's bad." For this reason the mind consciousness is especially important for us as human beings.

For as long as we circle within samsara, the mind consciousness plays the most important part in this. It is also extremely important in terms of our dharma practice. When, for example, we visualize a deity, from whose perspective do we meditate? It is not the eye consciousness that meditates on the form, because the five sense consciousnesses cannot meditate. It is the mind consciousness that meditates, in so much as it brings the form to consciousness. When we know this, we understand why it is that during the meditation on a deity the visualization does not appear so clearly. Mind does not take an object directly; instead, it perceives its own self-created mental images of the apprehended objects. Thus, whether your visualization is clear or not depends on the stability of your mind.

Some meditators think that they have to visualize as clearly as when the eye perceives something. However, the object will not be so clear, since it is not the eye that meditates. The eye consciousness is thought-free. It is not in the least able to meditate on a deity. It merely perceives what is in its sight, but it cannot 'visualize' as such. It is the mind consciousness that visualizes the deity. While the mind consciousness is meditating there is no real external object, as is the case when the eye perceives forms. Nevertheless, there is a kind of image of the object that appears to the mind consciousness. This image is created by the mind itself. As soon as the mind wavers, the object that it has created will change as well and at once be unstable. That's why we cannot visualize clearly while the mind is unstable. When the mind becomes more stable it is able to keep the self-created appearances longer. When the mind creates the appearance of a deity freshly and is not stable while doing so, this appearance will almost immediately vanish as soon as it arises. If the mind is a bit more stable, however, this reflection will remain for much longer. Whether the visualization of the deity in our meditation is clear or not depends solely on the stability of our mind. And this is exactly what we are training in when we meditate on a deity.

In the meditation on calm abiding also, it is not the five sense consciousnesses that meditate, but the mind consciousness. Some practitioners believe that when they constantly see objects with their eyes while meditating on calm abiding, their meditation is impaired, or that when they perceive sounds with their ears, their meditation will not be that beneficial. However, the five sense consciousnesses are not in the least able to create anything; therefore they cannot distract our mind either. The eyes indeed see forms, but it doesn't matter. Likewise the ears hear sounds, and the nose perceives smells, yet this does not disturb the meditation in the least, because the sense perception does not involve any thoughts. It is only a matter of mere appearances. This is the reason why we do not have to stop them. We would not even be able to stop them, nor do we have to modify anything in any way. The sense perception just happens naturally, by itself.

Then what is it that we have to do? While the mind consciousness meditates on calm abiding, it moves wildly. In moving it remembers the past, thinks ahead of the future, or finds itself within the present. It is shaken by many different thoughts: thoughts of happiness, thoughts of suffering, and many other kinds. When the mind does not continuously change in this way, but has instead become stable and is able to rest within itself, then it can be said that we remain within the meditative concentration of calm abiding.

Now, there are some sceptical persons who may think that when the mind is not moved by many thoughts, it will be in a stupid state. But stupidity does not arise just because the mind relaxes a little. On the contrary, the mind usually thinks too much. We are used to thinking uninterruptedly and continuously. If we look at these thoughts more closely, however, we discover that we seldom think meaningfully at all, and that most of our thinking is rather senseless. Such senseless thinking happens frequently and repeats itself over and over. In this way our many endlessly occurring thoughts are continuously going around and around in circles. If we are able to decrease this senseless thinking, meaningful thoughts will naturally increase all by themselves. And this is exactly the reason for the meditation on calm abiding: when the mind relaxes, senseless thinking will effortlessly diminish.

All of the six consciousnesses apprehend objects; therefore they are also called the 'six apprehending consciousnesses'. The five sense consciousnesses apprehend their respective objects directly, whereas the mind consciousness apprehends these indirectly and allows thoughts to arise. Thus the most important consciousness by far is the mind consciousness. It acts as the root for all attachment and aversion, all happiness and suffering. Thus it is as important for our daily life as it is for our meditation. For it is only the mind consciousness that can meditate. In the context of the three activities of Buddhist practice—namely listening, reflecting, and meditating—the mind consciousness plays the largest part. 'Listening' happens immediately after the arising of an ear consciousness which itself merely perceives the sounds of the words but which cannot itself connect the sounds to any meaning. 'Reflecting' about the meaning of the words is undertaken solely by the mind consciousness, which is also responsible for 'meditating'.

Thus the six collections of consciousness constitute two different categories of consciousness, each with different defining characteristics. There are the five sense consciousnesses that clearly perceive and have direct contact with the object. And then there is the mind consciousness that merely perceives its own self-created images of these objects, and therefore these objects appear as vague, wavering, or unclear.

Another difference between the five sense consciousnesses and the mind consciousness concerns time. The sense consciousnesses can only perceive in the very present moment, whereas the mind consciousness can think about the past, the present, and the future. Buddhist scholars use the following simile: "The five sense consciousnesses are like a mute with good eyes." They perceive clearly, but are not able to express themselves or to 'talk' about what something actually looks like nor what indeed it is that they perceive. The quote continues: "The thoughts are like blind persons who are gifted speakers." This refers to the mind consciousness which, although it only perceives the objects in a vague and unclear way, 'talks' a lot about them, commenting with its many thoughts on the vaguely perceived objects like a well-gifted speaker.

Chapter Two
THE STABLE CONSCIOUSNESSES

The five sense consciousnesses and the mind consciousness are not stable, because sometimes they arise and then they vanish, only to freshly arise again and again. As soon as we open our eyes the eye consciousness arises, but when we close our eyes it is not possible for the eye consciousness to arise. When we open our eyes again, it will arise again. When—in stormy weather, for example—we hear the sound of thunder, it means that an ear consciousness has arisen. As soon as the sound fades away, the corresponding ear consciousness vanishes. With the next sound of thunder another ear consciousness would arise afresh.

The stable consciousnesses, however, work differently. They are uninterruptedly present and function continuously while we are walking or sitting, whether we are distracted or concentrated, while we sleep or we work, and even during a fainting fit or being anesthetized.[17] Whenever it may be, the clear essence of mind, the essence that retains memories clearly, never dissolves. That's why these kinds of consciousness are called the stable consciousnesses.

The two kinds of stable consciousness include the klesha-mind (literally, the mind endowed with afflictions)[18] and the all-base consciousness.

THE KLESHA-MIND

Though the klesha-mind is characterized as the 'mind endowed with afflictions', it does not include all of the mental afflictions. Desirous attachment, anger, dullness, or similar afflictions are not referred to here, but only those that are included in the category of 'holding on to a self'. These can be divided into two kinds: holding on to the self of the person and holding on to the self of phenomena.

The first of these appears in the form of the thought "I": this is exactly what the klesha-mind is. When occasionally the conception of an 'I' is very gross, this is not a function of the klesha-mind, but has instead to do with the sixth consciousness, the mind consciousness. The thoughts of the klesha-mind are not very clear to us. They consist of us continuously thinking of and holding onto an 'I'. It is a case of the most utterly subtle conception of an 'I', comparable to someone who continuously thinks "I" without ever for an instant forgetting it. These rigid and inflexible thoughts of self-cherishing arise involuntarily.

Since the klesha-mind's subtle conception of an 'I' is never interrupted—no matter what we are doing—it is, as is the case with the all-base consciousness, classified as a stable consciousness. The klesha-mind's continuous and uninterrupted thinking of an 'I' is always accompanied by subtle mental events. It is not only the mere conception of an 'I' that is just thinking "I"; in addition there is the unnoticed thought "I am important," which is the 'attachment to the I'. Simultaneously the conception of an 'I' admits of ignorance and haziness, because the 'I' is not realized as being false.[19] Furthermore, the klesha-mind is suffused by a subtle pride that generally expresses itself in the thought "I am better than others." These four mental events—the conception of an 'I', the attachment to the 'I', ignorance, and pride—continuously accompany the klesha-mind; this is why it is called 'the mind endowed with afflictions'. It serves as the basis for the mind consciousness to build up the coarse grasping at a self, the force of which increases more and more.

Usually, mind is divided into the principal mind and mental events.[20] Generally speaking, the eight collections of consciousness belong to the principal mind, which means the klesha-mind does as well. It is, however, continuously accompanied by the above-mentioned mental events. In this context the 'subtle conception of an I' is also designated as the 'view of the conception of an I'. It is called 'view' in order to indicate that it includes a slight aspect of clarity.[21]

The afflictions of desirous attachment, anger, and dullness are compounded of negative thoughts. The affliction grasping at a self, however, is not a negative thought, but instead a neutral one. It is the continuous attachment of thinking "That's me," and that thought is neither positive nor negative. It is not a question of negativity nor of virtue; nevertheless, grasping at a self can bring about the states of negativity or virtue. It is the cause for all positive and negative actions. In its own essence, however, grasping at a self is neutral.

In this context we can differentiate two kinds of neutrality. In any case, 'neutral' means neither positive nor negative. However, something can indeed be neutral but still obscure the level of liberation, in which case it is called both 'obscuring and neutral'. The klesha-mind, that is, our grasping at a self, is generally considered neutral. Nevertheless, it is a hindrance to attaining liberation. Though its essence is not negative, it does, however, obscure the ultimate fruition; hence it is 'obscuring and neutral'. 'Non-obscuring and neutral' is used to describe anything that is neutral and does not cause any obscurations to liberation as, for example, walking back and forth, sitting or any other kind of ordinary behavior of this type.

In our present situation, that of being an ordinary person, the klesha-mind, as a stable consciousness, is permanently present, no matter what we are doing, whether we are sleeping or awake. Besides, there will come a point in time when it will be abandoned.

Let's first look at the noble ones (Skt. *arya*)[22] of the first bodhisattva level. The moment they see the truth of dharmata directly, the klesha-mind is not present because what they are realizing is the nonexistence of a self. They've got a vastly clear appearance of the nonexistence of a self. At this moment the klesha-mind stops functioning. However, through the power of their karmic imprints the klesha-mind appears again when they don't meditate. This is why their klesha-mind is still present during their post-meditational phase. From the point of view of the path of the hearers (Skt. *shravaka*),[23] during the attainment of arhatship the nonexistence of a self of the person is totally realized, both within meditation as well as outside, during post-meditation. Thus, when a hearer achieves arhatship the klesha-mind is totally abandoned. From the point of view of the great vehicle (Skt. *mahayana*), the klesha-mind is totally abandoned on the eighth bodhisattva level. At this point it totally transforms, and above the eighth level it no longer exists as such.

It is very important to understand the actual way of being of the klesha-mind. Since its essence is neutral, this is precisely why, in spite of grasping at a self, it is possible to temporarily accumulate what is called 'defiled virtue'.[24] From the ultimate point of view, however, the klesha-mind has to be abandoned, because grasping at a self is the root of all mental afflictions—all of which, in turn, must obviously be abandoned. Abandoning the afflictions coincides with the abandonment of grasping at a self.[25]

The All-Base Consciousness

The last of the eight collections of consciousness is the all-base consciousness. It is the second of the stable consciousnesses. The all-base consciousness is the general basis for the whole mind, and thus for all of the consciousnesses.

Though each of the particular consciousnesses has its own specific functions and defining characteristics, you can, from the absolute point of view, only talk of the mind as a singularity. The mind is one; its essence is one. It has its specific defining characteristics and functions, but only a single expression which is clear and cognizing. When the eyes see an object and the mind immediately apprehends that object without having to check or confirm it through any other process, or, when the mind consciousness understands the ear consciousness immediately, a connection of mutuality is indicated. Though the mind is divided into particular categories, the connection comes about due to the single nature of the all-base consciousness. Being the basis for all aspects of the mind, it is designated as the eighth consciousness.

The all-base consciousness expresses itself in two different ways. Firstly, it is the 'all-base that seizes karmic imprints'. That means all karmic imprints, such as the perceptions of the eyes, ears, nose, tongue, or those of the body, as well as all mental activities including those of a studious nature, are grasped by the all-base so that they will not be forgotten. In this way memories are made: something is seized and not thereafter forgotten. None of the consciousnesses of the six collections can seize their imprints. These consciousnesses dissolve as soon as they arise. However, the corresponding karmic imprints are stored within the all-base. They are collected there, and thus not forgotten. If we learn something today the corresponding information is stored in the form of karmic imprints within the all-base, and this is why it is possible to remember it tomorrow or at a later date. In this respect—that of the functions of seizing, storing, and not thereafter forgetting—the all-base consciousness is called the 'all-base that seizes karmic imprints'.

The second aspect of the all-base consciousness is called the 'all-base of complete ripening'.[26] This designates the possibility of allowing the karmic imprints that were once stored in the mind to reappear again. The future reappearance of the karmic imprints is the function of the all-base of complete ripening. Generally, as is the case for perception, it seems as if the sense organs and their corresponding faculties were located inside the body and the perceived objects outside. We take it for granted that, for example, the eye and the eye faculty are inside and the perceived form, the eye object, outside. While we are engaged in the act of seeing, the eye seems to look at the object, a form that is present outside. We therefore think that forms, sounds, smells, tastes, and tangible objects are externally present and that their corresponding consciousnesses are internal. From the Buddhist point of view this is certainly not the case. In our view the eye consciousness merely perceives a mental image of the form to be perceived. This form is not really external, but merely mental.[27] The same is the case for all other sense objects; the mind itself appears in their form. Other than that they don't exist externally at all.[28] Therefore we teach that all appearances are mind. If we ask ourselves how the objects appear, we can say that it is the all-base consciousness itself that appears in the form of these objects, which are then perceived through the perspective of the sense consciousnesses. This is why this aspect is called the 'all-base of complete ripening'.

When we teach that all appearances are just appearances of the mind, it often happens that beginners cannot put their trust in that. This is because our karmic imprints have been stored since beginningless time, one of which is the assumption that the sense objects are external and the mind internal. With precisely this imprint we have a difficult time understanding that the objects appear as an image of the mind. In order to clarify this point through careful analysis, we can take dreaming as an example. In the context of a dream mountains, houses, horses, elephants, and so forth appear to us, and we take it for granted that these appearances are actually present externally. We think that the mountain is actually there. The same is valid for the house in a dream: we think it is really present. In reality, however, there does not exist the slightest trace of any house or mountain. They are not actually there, but still they appear as if they were.

So where is it that they appear? They appear in the essence of the mind. Since every one of us has our individual experiences in dreams, it is easy for us to understand that the dream objects merely appear within the mind. As with the dream objects, in this example, the same applies to the whole of reality while we are not dreaming. We assume the appearances of objects in ordinary life, when we are not dreaming, are indubitably there. However, they are not truly present externally. They appear on the basis of the inner mind, in the same way as appearances in a dream. The karmic imprints once stored in the all-base reawake, emerge, and appear to us.

The all-base consciousness works like a savings bank. Continuously money is paid into the bank and continuously it is taken out again. In the same way karmic imprints are absorbed by the all-base, are stored there, and can therefore be brought forth again. Learning, for example, occurs through the mind consciousness. The mind consciousness itself vanishes. Nevertheless, on the next day we have a memory of what we learned. At this time of remembrance, the mind consciousness of what we learned is no longer actually present, since it has ceased to exist. Yet, still we did not forget what we learned previously. What we learned was seized by the all-base in the form of karmic imprints, and stored. Due to the 'all-base of complete ripening' these imprints can be re-awakened, so that the mind consciousness perceives them afresh. This is why we learn things. It is similar with strong mental afflictions. When one day we have a fight, it can happen that the anger is still raging the day after. This is because the karmic imprints of the anger were stored in the all-base and are raised to consciousness again the next day. Thus all karmic actions cause a future result on the basis of the all-base consciousness's capacity to store and to bring forth.

The example of the savings bank is particularly effective, especially in the context of karmic actions. Whoever puts money into the bank can get it out again later, often including interest! In the case of karma, we can see that even from a small karmic action it is possible to reap a heavy consequence. Though the cause may be small, the result is often large, or heavier.

Once the imprints of our actions are stored in the all-base, it is sometimes possible that a long period of time elapses before the result shows itself. Sometimes, however, only a little time is needed. The result can ripen in two ways: as the 'result in accordance with the cause' and as the 'completely ripened result'. As for the 'result in accordance with the cause', the causal action is similar to the later experienced result. If, for example, we are angry, a greater anger may later be the result. Or, should a person develop compassion, this compassion can increase more and more. This is due to the power of the karmic imprints. As for the 'completely ripened result' of our actions, it is a reply to the causal action. If we are nasty to another person, as a reply, later, we will experience nastiness inflicted upon ourselves. This, also, is due to the power of karmic imprints.

The completely ripened result of an action can express itself in four different ways. If we have got an intensely strong intention and act accordingly, this is said to be a 'karmic action with the result being experienced in this life'. This means that, when we act virtuously we will experience the positive result with our present body of this life. Whoever commits negative actions will experience the corresponding negative result within this life. In other cases, however, the fruit might not ripen within this life but within the next. Then it is a case of 'karmic actions with the result experienced after rebirth'. It can also happen that the result is neither experienced in this life nor in the next, but at some time thereafter, when the right causes and conditions come together. This means that in some future life, at some time or other, the result will show. This is called a 'karmic action with the experience of the result after an uncertain number [of rebirths]'. If the causal action has even less power than this, it is uncertain whether the result will be experienced at all. If it is very weak, it is possible that the result is lost entirely due to other, stronger conditions. In this instance it is a case of a 'karmic action with uncertainty over the experience of a result'. In all these cases the karmic imprints are stored in the all-base and can come out in all these various ways.

Even while meditating, karmic imprints are formed. Within calm abiding the sixth consciousness, the mind consciousness, relaxes. While doing that, however, it still continues to function. Even if the mind rests in total calm, the stream of its clarity aspect is uninterrupted; only the coarse thoughts are calming down. One can compare the mind consciousness to waves and the all-base consciousness to the ocean. In the same way that the waves arise from the ocean, the mind consciousness emerges from the all-base. When the waves collapse and smoothen out, the ocean becomes quiet. This corresponds to the relaxed abiding of the mind consciousness within the all-base. All the coarse thoughts have become calm. Nevertheless, we do not meditate like a stone, for the clarity aspect of mind that knows and understands everything is never interrupted. Due to this reason the mind is clear and radiant, even when it rests within the all-base.

In the case of deity meditation, it is the mind consciousness that creates the body of the deity. It is thus a mentally created body, and thus, so to speak, unreal. When, however, the karmic imprints of this visualization get stored in the all-base and become more clear and more stable, it is actually possible to meet the deity one day, or Guru Rinpoche, for example, face to face! This is the result of deity meditation with in-front visualization.

As for self-visualization, we meditate on ourselves as being the deity. In the beginning this thought—that we ourselves are the deity, or for example Guru Rinpoche, is unreal as well. However, when the karmic imprints of that become more stable, the mind, primordial awareness, compassion, and all the innate qualities of Guru Rinpoche will manifest within ourselves. This is so because we *already* have these qualities within our mind. They are just temporarily obscured, and the obscurations can be removed step by step through meditation. Eventually these qualities will reappear, pure and clear, out of the all-base. This is the result of deity meditation using the method of self-visualization.

Thus all the karmic imprints are stored within the mind. This is also true of the imprints of our dharma practice. Whoever is able to practice the true dharma in a perfect way will soon reach the ultimate result. If, however, we are not able to practice in such a perfect way—for example, when we only practice occasionally—the karmic imprints will not get lost, because they are also stored within the mind, i.e., the all-base. They function like a rooted seed that will grow bit by bit. Some practitioners think that their practice does not manifest any results; nevertheless, just carrying this seed of practice is very beneficial.

This was taught by Buddha Shakyamuni in the sutras. In this context he taught that even practicing only a small act of dharma activity is beneficial. When he was asked whether it was beneficial to show your respect by just raising one hand instead of folding both in a gesture of prayer, he explained that ultimately the level of buddhahood can be reached through doing only that. The reason for the attainment of such an unsurpassable result is not the raising of one hand—there is no inherent benefit in this—but it is the karmic imprint of respect that is stored within the all-base, and therefore is able to increase more and more without getting lost. This is why the ultimate fruit of buddhahood can result from just a small act of dharma activity.

Chapter Three
THE MENTAL EVENTS

According to the Buddhist view, mind is described in two divisions: the principal mind, and mental events. The principal mind encompasses the eight collections of consciousness as previously explained. These are called 'collections' because they consist of a multiplicity. This means that the eye consciousness, for example, is already a 'collection' in itself. It is not single and separate. Though its essence seems to be single, it still consists of a multiplicity of aspects of consciousness. Looking at a piece of colored cloth, we experience many moments of consciousness per se, just based on the eye consciousness itself. One moment of consciousness of the color yellow arises, one of the color red, one of the color blue, and so on. There arises a moment of consciousness of each and every visual detail. Thus there can be no single all-encompassing eye consciousness. The same is true of all the other sense consciousnesses. The mind consciousness also is not single, but likewise a multiplicity of different aspects of consciousness. This becomes very obvious with time, because time changes automatically from moment to moment. The same is true of the klesha-mind and also of the all-base consciousness. The reason for emphasizing the multiplicity of the consciousnesses by calling them 'collections' is that the mind in itself is easily mistaken for the self. Mind is easily seized as the self. Such a self manifests in two different ways: as 'spontaneously present self' and as 'completely imputed self'.

The 'spontaneously present self' is the automatic, perpetual grasping at a self by thinking "I"; it is innate in all of us. Sometimes we refer to this self as being our body, and sometimes as being our mind. With this aspect of the spontaneously present self the assumption arises that the self is single.

The truly existent self that is asserted by the followers of some non-Buddhist religions—for example, by the Indian Tirthikas—corresponds to the 'completely imputed self'. From their point of view mind *is* the self: it is single and permanent. We Buddhists, however, know that in reality mind is neither single nor permanent. Its nature is a variety of different aspects of consciousness. Mind is composed of eight kinds of consciousness, each of which is a collection. For this reason, mind is emphasized as being the eight 'collections' of consciousness, which thus points towards the nonexistence of a self.

Generally speaking, the principal mind can see, cognize, understand, and appear, all due to its clarity aspect. Nevertheless, whenever the actual clarity aspect becomes more intense, and when the particular details are also clearly perceived, this induces the process of mental events.[29] Buddha Shakyamuni explained these mainly in the abhidharma teachings, in which he describes fifty-one mental events, also known as 'mental formations'. Though in some cases there are more than that, in general we speak of fifty-one.

If you summarize these, there are five categories of mental events. The first category comprises the 'ever-present mental events'. Ever-present means that the continuous activity of the mind and the appearance of all the various aspects of consciousness that keep the whole mind moving cause an uninterrupted appearance of sensations. Thus we continuously experience mental events, such as the sensations of our own happiness or suffering. For this reason they are called ever-present.[30]

The second category comprises the 'mental events with certainty over the object'. These events do not appear the moment the consciousness appears, but only when one has developed certainty or assurance of the object. They only appear when the object is perceived clearly and with stability, and usually within the context of the five sense consciousnesses and the mind consciousness.[31]

The third category comprises the 'virtuous mental events'. These are your own positive attitudes, arising together with virtuous actions. They neither appear in the context of the five sense consciousnesses nor in that of the all-base or klesha-mind. Instead they follow the sixth consciousness, the mind consciousness.[32]

Then there are the mental events which belong to the collection of mental afflictions. These are also divided into two kinds: the 'root afflictions' and the 'secondary afflictions'. The root afflictions are the constant and more intense afflictions, whereas the secondary afflictions appear only occasionally. These two kinds of mental afflictions describe the impure aspect of the mind, while the virtuous mental events describe its pure aspect.[33]

The fifth category comprises the 'variable mental events'. Since these can sometimes turn into virtuous states, and sometimes into negative states, they are said to be variable.[34]

The mental events come into play alongside the operation of the principal mind. When the principal mind is consumed by many strong thoughts, they appear much more frequently. When the thoughts are weak, only a few mental events will appear. If the root and secondary afflictions are enumerated separately, one can also speak of 'the six categories of the thoughts of mental events'. Summarized further, however, they can be divided into five, and are also designated as the fifty-one mental formations. Within deity meditation their presence is denoted symbolically. The completely purified mental events are visualized—for example, in the meditation on Vajravarahi (Dorje Pagmo)—in the form of her necklaces. One necklace is made of fifty-one flowers and the other of fifty-one skulls. In the Nyingma meditation on the peaceful and wrathful deities, the completely pure mental events are meditated upon in the form of the fifty-one wrathful deities in our brain.[35]

Upon the basis of the principal mind with its division into the eight collections of consciousness and the fifty-one mental events, there arise the delusion-based appearances of samsara. Thus, it is due to the mind that karmic imprints are collected. Sometimes these are positive karmic imprints that contribute to a positive development. Sometimes these are negative karmic imprints that contribute to a negative development. The direction of one's development is fundamentally dependent on one's own conditions; principally, however, it depends on one's own motivation. For this reason we meditate and accumulate virtue so that all emerging appearances improve, and so that impurity is given up gradually and transformed into purity. The peak of this transformation is the transformation of what is impure, i.e., the eight kinds of consciousness, into what is pure, i.e., the five kinds of primordial awareness that are also designated as 'primordial awareness of the perfect Buddhas' great compassion'. Such a transformation is possible because the appearances are not truly existent externally, but are in fact internal. This means they are appearances of one's own inner mind. Whoever has gained control over his/her mind is able to transform the impure appearances into pure appearances. In this way we can have an aim to strive for and to attain.

From the Buddhist point of view this is how the mind functions. Modern Western psychology also concerns itself with similar phenomena. For example, it is said that anger may be suppressed, and if it is not released, it can cause problems. This means one hides one's anger inside, which corresponds to the Buddhist description of the storage of karmic imprints within the all-base. The main difference, however, is the way the problem is treated: in Buddhist terms, we call this the way of purification. From the Buddhist point of view karmic imprints are stored in the mind, i.e., the all-base, and for this reason, exactly, they may be purified through meditation. In this way the meditator gains control over the mind. Through the meditation of calm abiding, for example, the mind becomes more and more independent. Once the mind is independent, even the most subtle karmic imprints cannot cause harm. A different approach is the meditation of deep insight, through which we come to understand that the essence of mind is naturally empty. And, when this naturally empty but clear essence of mind is realized, karmic imprints likewise cannot cause harm. Western psychology uses different methods to purify the 'karmic imprints', but the corresponding understanding of where these are stored indicates that we are not that dissimilar in view.

Chapter Four
MEDITATION INVOLVING THE CONSCIOUSNESSES

The teachings on the eight collections of consciousness and the five kinds of primordial awareness are particular to Buddhist philosophy which, on the one hand, clearly presents the way we are trapped in the situation of cyclic existence, and, on the other, how it is possible to fully manifest the primordial awarenesses in future through progression on the path.

Most world religions try to bring people to practice positive conduct of body, speech, and mind. Buddhism does likewise; thus, all religions for the most part agree on what constitutes virtuous behavior. Differences remain, however, concerning the view. Many religions that have spread in China, India, or the West assert, in one way or another, a god as the creator of the world. The conduct of such believers towards their god then determines their future situation. They will be rewarded for positive behavior and called to account for negative behavior.

Buddhism does not promulgate anything like that. From the Buddhist point of view, all appearances are nothing other than delusion-based, and their karmic imprints are stored in the all-base. Due to the reappearance of these imprints it is possible for all the different appearances and all the different thoughts of mind to arise. It is a stream of karmic imprints that arises within ourselves. Whoever is able to traverse the truly authentic path can purify his or her mind of negative karmic imprints and thus eventually transform all aspects of delusion. In this way the five kinds of primordial awareness arise as purified manifestations from the eight kinds of consciousness. This is the ultimate aim of the Buddhist path. For this reason the eight collections of consciousness act as an underlying basis for the view of the Buddhist tradition. The possibility of purification of these eight consciousnesses and their transformation into primordial awareness is the reason why meditation is necessary. Thus the Buddhist view self-evidently teaches the ultimate result to be reached and the path that leads to that fruit, i.e., meditation. In addition, it teaches how we are deluded without practicing meditation.

The causes for happiness and joy are dependent on the mind, as is also the cause for suffering. Through the right training we are able to transform the mind, that is, the eight collections of consciousness, into primordial awareness. This transformation is possible because the intrinsic essence of mind is already primordial awareness. Only through meditation can this fruit be manifested.

Nowadays many people meditate, both in the West and the East, and the methods of calm abiding and deep insight are two fairly well-known types of meditation. In the practice of calm abiding there are many meditation methods that are based on breathing. These are very effective in hindering the arising of many thoughts. This was originally taught by Buddha Shakyamuni, who said, "When there are quite a lot of thoughts, you should meditate by concentrating on your breathing."[36] Sometimes it is also beneficial to use one of the many other types of methods associated with calm abiding according to your own personal requirements.

Having explained the eight collections of consciousness above, I will now present a useful meditation method of the practice of calm abiding which involves the consciousnesses. It accords with what Wangchug Dorje, the Ninth Karmapa, taught in his meditation manuals of the great seal

(Skt. *mahamudra*), *Ocean of Definitive Meaning* and *Pointing Out the Dharmakaya.*

First, the meditation involving the eye consciousness: The eyes continuously look at forms. This leads to the possibility of two kinds of focal direction in your meditation. You can either focus on an impure or a pure object of meditation. The impure object could be a small stone or a piece of wood that we place in our field of vision. As mentioned previously, the eye consciousness does not meditate. Immediately after it has perceived its object, thoughts arise through the medium of the mind consciousness. At this point we use the focused concentration of the eye consciousness on the stone or on the wood in order to keep the mind quiet and tranquil. The eye consciousness continues to look at the object, neither too tensely nor too loosely. This is an act of mere seeing. The stone or the wood is *merely* perceived without our giving rise to thoughts about form, shape, color, and so forth. In this way we could look at any form that attracts our eye consciousness. The mind consciousness is meant to follow the focus of the eye consciousness and is thus held at one point. One-pointedness of mind is attained through merely not forgetting the focal object. This meditation is called 'holding the mind based on the eye consciousness with an impure object as a focus'.

To use a pure object for the concentration of the eye consciousness, we should place a small buddha statue into our field of vision. A buddha statue is considered a 'pure' object because, in general, it inspires faith and devotion towards the Buddha. For this meditation to succeed, however, it does not matter whether we develop faith or trust or not; the statue merely serves as the focal object for the undistracted concentration of our eye consciousness and to help the mind concentrate by merely not forgetting. While meditating like this, different kinds of meditation experiences may arise. When the clarity aspect of mind increases due to this meditation, it can easily lead to distraction. In this instance, we should direct our mind towards the lower parts of the statue, the lotus seat for example. If dullness and haziness arise, we should concentrate our consciousness towards the upper part of the statue, either towards the head or towards the Buddha's hair knot. These meditation methods are designated as 'holding the mind based on the eye consciousness'.

For beginners new to meditation it is important to meditate initially just for a short time. In order to 'set your mind'[37] correctly you need awareness and mindfulness with which you neither stray away from the object of focus nor are too tight. When you are able to rest like this, with a stable and clear mind, you may extend the meditation slightly which then is called 'continuous setting'.[38] When, in such a meditation, the mind is distracted by other thoughts and drawn back again from that distraction, we talk of 'resetting the mind'.[39] It happens a lot that within meditation you think, "Oh, my mind no longer rests on the object of focus." If one recognizes this distraction with such a thought of awareness and continues the meditation once again, this is what is meant by resetting the mind. Distraction is not good, but it's definitely not bad either, it just happens! If one manages to come back to the object of focus, the original meditation is reset on the correct course. These ways of setting the mind can be applied generally to any meditation involving the consciousnesses.

Secondly, the mind can be held based on using the ear consciousness. The ear consciousness perceives sounds. If, however, there is no sound, no ear consciousness can arise. During this type of meditation the ear consciousness is directed towards a sound. Simultaneously one holds one's mind consciousness undistractedly on the same object of focus. This is called 'holding the mind based on the ear consciousness'.

As for holding the mind based on the nose consciousness we must also, first of all, just watch its functioning. Sometimes it apprehends intense smells, sometimes those that are less intense. Smells can be sweet, sour or various. If the mind consciousness concentrates on the smell uninterruptedly and undistractedly, then this is what is called 'holding the mind based on the nose consciousness'. Even though the mind consciousness tends to apprehend the smell by means of thoughts, it should not stray to other objects in any way whatsoever. The smell alone must be held conceptually; one must not allow oneself to think about anything else. The apprehender of the smell is the sixth consciousness, the mind consciousness. This is the thinker. The method to hold the mind, however, is to focus the nose consciousness on a smell.

The same is valid for the tongue consciousness. When we eat something we experience a very intense taste. Even without eating, a fine and subtle sense of taste still exists. This is what the sixth consciousness, the mind consciousness, has to seize very carefully. The tongue consciousness continuously experiences a subtle taste. This subtle taste is what the mind has to be concentrated on without distraction.

The body consciousness apprehends physically tangible objects. Sometimes these may be strong feelings of touch. But even though no such feeling may be there, the body apprehends continuously a fine and pleasant physical sensation. This is experienced from the head to the toes over the whole body. In this meditation we concentrate our mind consciousness precisely on this perception without once forgetting this feeling. In this way we hold the mind. This concludes the description of the meditation involving the five sense consciousnesses.

As for the meditation based on the sixth, the mind consciousness itself, there are two possibilities: 'holding the mind with a focus' and 'holding the mind without any focus'. The following kinds of visualization are also taken from the above-mentioned meditation manuals by Wangchug Dorje.

As for 'holding the mind with a focus', we imagine a white, a red, and a blue drop in the space in front of us. The mind consciousness should clearly visualize these, in the same way as one visualizes the form of the creation-stage practice.[40] One's own mind itself creates these three drops in order to concentrate on them later on without distraction. In this way the mind consciousness is held one-pointedly on this focus.

For beginners new to meditation it is usually much more pleasant to close the eyes while visualizing. However, the more often this visualization is repeated and the less distractedly you concentrate your mind, the easier it becomes to visualize the three drops clearly, even with open eyes.

While meditating with a focus the mind consciousness necessarily entertains a certain conceptual activity. While meditating without a focus, on the other hand, you simply let your mind relax. There is no object of focus at all, neither one based on the five senses nor on any kind of mental image. Nevertheless, the mind consciousness and the five sense consciousnesses are not switched either. Instead, you allow the sixth consciousness, the mind consciousness, to relax, so that it is not possible for either positive or negative thoughts to arise. In this case, the clarity aspect of mind is not interrupted. Because of its continuous clarity aspect the mind indeed perceives everything; it is just that the rough thoughts, such as "I went here" or "I remember this," dissolve.

Two mental events play a big role in this meditation. On the one hand one needs mindfulness, through the application of which one does not forget that one is meditating; on the other hand, one needs alertness which is continuously present and aware of what the mind is doing. Within this type of meditation mindfulness and alertness are applied loosely while the mind itself relaxes. While relaxing like this the mind's clarity aspect is not interrupted; nevertheless, the coarse thoughts do not appear. Allowing the mind to relax and its clarity aspect to function in this way is called 'holding the mind without a focus or without a basis'.

Whereas the mind consciousness is involved in each meditation, the seventh consciousness, the klesha-mind, is not. From within the eight collections of consciousness the klesha-mind is the only consciousness for which there is no meditation method at all.

The all-base consciousness plays its role in the meditation as well. When the mind rests calmly within equipoise and meditates, when it relaxes and becomes stable, and when there arise barely any thoughts, then the mind consciousness rests within the mere clarity aspect of the all-base. Through relaxing the mind, mind consciousness and the all-base consciousness rest together in the mere, continuous clarity aspect of mind. The clarity aspect of mind is an unfabricated cognition, a mere perception—the true nature of mind. The true nature of mind is the uninterrupted clarity aspect. When the coarse thoughts of the mind consciousness are pacified, it comes to rest in the all-base, and both abide within the true nature of mind.

When the principal mind comes to rest through meditation, it is important to rely continuously on the two mental events of mindfulness and alertness. While the mind rests and is stable, mindfulness keeps the meditation on the correct course with the subtle thought, "I must rest in equipoise." If the meditation is not accompanied by such mindfulness, it may often seem to the meditators that their resting is stable; in fact, however, they do not notice that they became distracted long ago! In our meditation we often think, "I am resting within natural meditative concentration (Skt. *samadhi*)." But this is a thought, which is soon followed by many others, and we discover that we were distracted a long time previously. This is why our mindfulness serves as a watchman. Though it is said that mind is not split into two—that is, a watcher and something to be watched—we still need to keep our mindfulness alert constantly like a watchman.

At the same time we also need alertness, otherwise the mind gets lost in sensations through such thoughts as,

"What did I think this morning?" or, "What did I think there-after?" Alertness contains a clarity aspect that cognizes and is conscious of what happens in the mind in the form of subtle thoughts such as, "Now my mind is resting in equipoise," "Now a thought came up," "Now I remembered something." This is called alertness. Within our meditation we have to rely continuously on both, mindfulness and alertness.

Within meditation it can also happen that the mind relaxes so deeply that it becomes drowsy and thereby different kinds of appearances, forms, or colors appear. Such appearances are often mistaken for meditation experiences. However, these are not meditation experiences per se, but thoughts that arise in different forms due to the relaxed manner of the mind, out of which it is very easy for mental dullness and haziness to arise. In a situation like this, we should straighten up our body and exert it a little bit. Additionally we should exert the mind a bit more than before. In this way one strengthens the clarity aspect of mind and is able to rest within one's meditation again.

II
BUDDHA-AWAKENING

Chapter Five

THE FIVE KINDS OF PRIMORDIAL AWARENESS

If we want to reveal the primordial awarenesses, we need to understand their mode of being. Before we put the dharma into practice through meditation, we should first of all inform ourselves about what kind of results one can attain by doing so. Some people think that one attains an incredible multiplicity, others think that one attains a mere nothingness. Some hold the opinion that, through attaining such a positive level for oneself, all loving-kindness and compassion for others will be exhausted. Such mistaken assumptions about the results of meditation practice are all possible.

Through knowledge concerning the five kinds of primordial awareness and their essential self-nature, we can come to understand clearly what really occurs in the fruitional phase of the ultimate result. In addition, such knowledge enables us to practice the path of dharma in the correct way.

The ultimate fruit of dharma practice is the attainment of buddhahood. Liberating oneself from all ignorance, delusion, and obscurations, one manifests the qualities of a Buddha by attaining the five kinds of primordial awareness.

According to Jamgön Kongtrul Lodrö Thayé there are four causes for attaining primordial awareness: the highest understanding of listening, meditation on equality, teaching the dharma to others, and performing actions for the benefit of others.[41]

Listening and reflecting on the teachings of the true dharma give rise to the highest understanding with which we are able to comprehend correctly the true nature of the dharma. This kind of highest understanding constitutes the cause for the future attainment of the mirrorlike primordial awareness.

The meditation on the equality of oneself and others, which includes all sentient beings, is practiced, for example, in the meditation of mind-training (*lojong*). It constitutes the cause for the future attainment of the primordial awareness of equality.

When, out of our own interest, we study the three collections of the Buddha's talks[42] and understand them, later we will be able to communicate our knowledge to others. For this purpose it is necessary to precisely discriminate information—for example, why it is necessary to practice the dharma, the essence of the true dharma, and the way to put the true dharma into practice. This enables us to develop the capability of distinguishing, which, in turn, is the cause for the future attainment of the discriminating primordial awareness. However, teaching the dharma should be performed with a completely pure motivation.

With the primordial awareness that accomplishes all actions, the fourth of the awarenesses, all kinds of activities can be performed. For this reason, the cause of its future attainment is our current behavior, for example, the performance of activities with completely pure motivation through which we liberate others from their suffering, the performance of activities through which others attain happiness, and the performance of activities through which we are able to practice the dharma.

These are the four causes for our gradual attainment of the primordial awarenesses. Though in general there are five kinds of primordial awareness, since the primordial awareness of the dharmadhatu pervades all the others, only four causes for the attainment of primordial awareness are taught.

The five kinds of primordial awareness are often summarized into two: the 'primordial awareness that knows the

nature of reality exactly as it is'[43] and the 'primordial awareness that knows the nature of reality to its full extent'.[44]

For as long as we wander within the cyclic existence of
samsara our consciousness deludes itself in terms of its perceptions. As soon as we penetrate this delusion, we gain insight into the true nature and are able to see the emptiness
nature of all phenomena. This is the true nature, free from all
delusion, deception or affliction, just as it is. It is the exact
mode of being of all phenomena. Seeing the emptiness is seeing the dharmadhatu,[45] or seeing the true nature of all things.
This is also designated as the 'primordial awareness that
knows the nature of reality exactly as it is'. It corresponds to
the primordial awareness of the dharmadhatu.

Attaining the primordial awareness that knows the nature of reality exactly as it is, one liberates oneself of all delusion and knows how the delusion-based appearances arise
for all the other beings who wander within samsara. From
the individual perspective of such a liberated person there is
no delusion extant anymore. From the perspective of all the
other beings, however, delusion is indeed paramount. The
subtle understanding of the joy and happiness of some beings and the suffering of others, of the causes for their suffering and of the ways they can liberate themselves from their
suffering, is called the 'knowledge from the perspective of
the others'. This is also designated as the 'primordial awareness that knows the nature of reality to its full extent'. It
comprises all the other four kinds of primordial awareness.

These two primordial awarenesses constitute a general
basis for the division into the five kinds of primordial awareness that are attained through purifying the eight collections
of consciousness.

THE PRIMORDIAL AWARENESS OF THE DHARMADHATU

The primordial awareness of the dharmadhatu is designated
the 'first' primordial awareness, because it constitutes the
pure basis for the gradual enlightenment of the knowledge

aspect of all those to be trained. It corresponds to the primordial awareness that knows the nature of reality exactly as it is, and is no less than the transformation of the all-base consciousness itself.

All the various kinds of delusion-based appearances of samsara—both the external objects of perception as well as the inner, perceiving mind—appear due to the basis, which is the all-base consciousness itself. Though the outer objects of perception seem to be external, they are not really so. This is because they appear internally, as mere mental appearances. The same is valid for the sense objects that are to be perceived by the sense consciousnesses; they are internal, merely mental appearances. They appear on the basis of the all-base consciousness. For this reason they are not truly existent, but instead delusion-based appearances.[46] Freedom from this delusion is reality in its purified aspect. With the transformation of the all-base consciousness, delusion is abandoned and insight into the true nature, the dharmadhatu, the inherent nature of the completely pure aspect of the delusion-based appearances is attained. From our own point of view we then dwell in the meditative concentration of perfect peace and freedom from all mental projections. Since the self-appearances of the enlightened mind are completely pure, this awareness is called the 'primordial awareness of the dharmadhatu'. It is the primordial awareness that sees the true nature of all phenomena.

THE MIRRORLIKE PRIMORDIAL AWARENESS

Whosoever is endowed with the primordial awareness of the dharmadhatu has not even the slightest suffering—no afflictions, attachment, grasping, pride, jealousy, or anger. This is because, when all appearances have been purified, we see the true nature, the dharmadhatu, that is itself peace. While we ourselves are evenly abiding within it, we nevertheless know the complete mode of being of all sentient beings. This occurs on the basis of the mirrorlike primordial awareness, the transformation of the all-base. Here the image of a mirror is used as an example to symbolize the appearance of all things. A mirror has no thoughts, such as "This is good" or "This is bad." It completely reflects each and every thing, no matter whether it is positive or negative. The mirrorlike primordial awareness functions similarly: Though from one's own perspective everything appears completely pure, all appearances from the perspective of others (that is, all the limitless sentient beings that have not yet reached the level of a Buddha) appear as well. These beings succumb to the delusion-based appearances of samsara. On this basis their inner afflictions arise, such as anger, desirous attachment, or pride, through which in turn they experience all the various kinds of suffering. In spite of their mental afflictions and their sufferings, their true nature is never separated from the expanse of the dharma-dhatu. However, they do not know this, and due to this ignorance there appear all the multifarious forms of appearances. A Buddha also knows the diversities of appearances experienced in samsara by sentient beings.

It may seem that the simultaneous presence of the primordial awareness of the dharmadhatu and the mirrorlike primordial awareness is contradictory. That is, from the perspective of the first, a Buddha abides in peace without in the least having to suffer delusion-based appearances. From the perspective of the second, a Buddha knows all the delusion-based appearances. If these are completely pacified, however, how is it that one can know them? And, on the other hand, when one knows all of the delusion-based appearances, how is it possible to have them pacified?

This contradiction can be resolved with the help of the following example. A sleeping person experiencing the nightmare of a tiger wanting to devour him is panic-stricken. Another person, one who possesses extrasensory perception, looks at the dreamer and knows at once of what he is dreaming but nevertheless does not in the least develop any fear that the tiger might devour him. This is because this second person does not dream. Although he sees the tiger in the dream of the other, he knows that it is not a real tiger and therefore does not succumb to the delusion of the dream. From his own perspective there is no reason for fear to arise, since the tiger does not appear to him. Nevertheless, with his extrasensory perception he knows the whole existential context of the dreamer—that he sleeps, that he dreams of a tiger, that he takes this appearance to be true and thus is afraid. As in this example, in the same way, it is possible for a Buddha not to have the least fear, suffering, or difficulties arising from the perspective of the primordial awareness of the dharmadhatu. But, from the perspective of the mirror-like primordial awareness, a Buddha also knows all of the personal, delusion-based appearances of all sentient beings, their individual difficulties, their negative conditions, and their sufferings. This is the function of the mirrorlike primordial awareness of a Buddha.

The Primordial Awareness of Equality

In this way all appearances are like reflections in a mirror, and can be seen and realized as such. A Buddha, however, does not develop attachment to any appearances. He views them as equal due to the primordial awareness of equality, which is the transformation of the klesha-mind.

As previously mentioned, the klesha-mind comes into play in the form of our grasping at a self. In every situation it grasps at a self by thinking, "I." On the basis of the thought "I" arises the thought "others." This distinction induces all kinds of attachment, aversion, and indifference. Through training in meditative concentration the sensations of the klesha-mind are pacified, our grasping at a self is diminished, and thus our discrimination between self and others diminishes. Finally we view ourselves and sentient beings as being equal. We no longer differentiate. When the klesha-mind is transformed there are no longer such thoughts as

"I want to be happy" or "I don't care if other beings suffer." Everything is equal. A sensation of myself and others as equal arises. This is what is called the 'primordial awareness of equality'.

THE DISCRIMINATING PRIMORDIAL AWARENESS

An objection may be raised that within the equality of all phenomena errors might easily occur, as, for example, to confuse good and bad. This does not happen, however, because although a Buddha sees everything as equal he or she still knows everything specifically without mixing anything up, by way of his or her discriminating primordial awareness. For example, doctors need to be able to discriminate specifically: to a patient with headache they have to give headache medicine; if the patient has a stomach problem, they have to give medicine for the stomach. They must not make mistakes or work in a vague or imprecise manner. In the same way, the discriminating primordial awareness knows everything distinctly without mixing anything up or falling into the tiniest single mistake; it knows each phenomenon specifically. The discriminating primordial awareness is the transformation of the mind consciousness.

While still impure, the mind consciousness is responsible for the specific discriminations into good and bad, into happiness or suffering. Thus, the defining characteristics as well as the function of the discriminating primordial awareness and the mind consciousness are quite close. They differ, however, in their modes of knowing. The sixth consciousness, the mind consciousness, perceives in a deluded way, whereas the discriminating primordial awareness perceives in a non-deluded way because it arises simultaneously with the above-mentioned primordial awarenesses. The discriminating primordial awareness perceives specific individual differences without mixing up the perceptions.

THE PRIMORDIAL AWARENESS THAT ACCOMPLISHES ALL ACTIONS

Again, doubts may arise that, should the discriminating primordial awareness realize appearances specifically, it will in all probability be impossible for it to act or behave accordingly. This would mean that a Buddha would not be capable of performing enlightened activity in a perfect way. It could be argued that a Buddha's realization of both equality and of the dharmadhatu that is free from all delusion is so extremely enhanced as for it not to be possible to perform actions or enlightened activity within the sphere of heavily deluded sentient beings. However, this mistake does not occur, because the fifth of the primordial awarenesses is the primordial awareness that accomplishes all actions. This awareness perfects the enlightened activity of a Buddha. It is precisely because he realizes things specifically and seamlessly that a Buddha performs enlightened activity. He knows the specific sufferings of sentient beings—just what kind of physical or mental sufferings they have. He even knows what kind of dreaded events are likely to happen. At the same time he is acting and applying methods to liberate them from their sufferings.

This awareness is called the 'primordial awareness that accomplishes all actions' because it is able to perfectly accomplish activities. It is the simultaneous transformation of all the five sense consciousnesses, the eye, ear, nose, tongue, and body consciousnesses. In general, the five sense consciousnesses make a connection between the inner consciousness and the outer objects. And it is because the eye perceives form, the ears perceive sounds, and the nose experiences smells that we are able to perform activities. Due to the function of all the five sense consciousnesses we direct our activities outwards. In the same way a perfect Buddha is able to perform enlightened activity with all five primordial awarenesses after the five sense consciousnesses have been transformed.

THE ABODE OF THE PRIMORDIAL AWARENESSES

Now the question arises as to where the five primordial awarenesses actually abide. They are in fact located within every one of us. Buddha Shakyamuni taught that every being possessing a mind also possesses the consciousnesses. Possessing the consciousnesses, one is also endowed with their true nature, i.e., the five kinds of primordial awareness, and can therefore manifest them. Within all sentient beings, the five primordial awarenesses are present as a foundation. Thus, our consciousness gives us the possibility and the opportunity to manifest the five kinds of primordial awareness.

The Sanskrit term for primordial awareness is *jñana*, which designates the clarity aspect that realizes the true nature. Thus primordial awareness is endowed with a clarity aspect as well as an emptiness aspect. Through intense clinging to the manifestations of the clarity aspect the mind loses itself in that,[47] and thus the consciousness itself—*vijñana* in Sanskrit—seems to be much clearer than the clarity aspect of primordial awareness. In this way the delusion-based appearances arise and appear very densely. Since these are based on delusion, their essence is ignorance—due to which, in turn, mental afflictions and all the different kinds of suffering arise.

If we therefore ask ourselves what is necessary to liberate ourselves from mental afflictions and from suffering, there is no need to look for a so-called 'Buddha' or a so-called 'path' anywhere else than within ourselves. We have to discover our own true nature, and allow it to manifest clearly. For this reason we must first of all train in meditative concentration and put the dharma into practice. Through these methods the delusion-based appearances of the eight collections of consciousness are liberated and their non-deluded essence, the five kinds of primordial awareness, can manifest clearly.

For as long as we traverse the path, our meditation gradually helps us to abandon delusion. Our delusion occurs because we do not realize the emptiness aspect in the coexistent emergence of emptiness and clarity. Appearances do not truly exist; they are empty. This is precisely what we do not realize and thus we delude ourselves. For this reason, in meditation we principally generate the energy potential of the primordial awareness of the dharmadhatu.

In the beginning we will not be able to directly meditate involving the primordial awareness of the dharmadhatu. Therefore we must start applying the nature of dharmadhatu with steadfast conviction. We develop conviction through thinking, "This is the true nature of mind," "This is the true essence of dharmadhatu." In this way we mentally create the true nature of dharmadhatu and will gradually come to see it directly. Through direct seeing, the primordial awareness of the dharmadhatu arises and, upon its basis, automatically the other four primordial awarenesses as well. This is because, on the basis of the primordial awareness of the dharmadhatu, all of the eight collections of consciousness naturally transform into the five kinds of primordial awareness. Thus, in order to allow the primordial awareness of the dharmadhatu to arise, one mainly meditates on the true nature—that is, the essence of dharmadhatu—first of all utilizing the meditations of calm abiding and deep insight.

In order to direct one's mind to the authentic path, however, one sometimes trains one's mind in the general preliminaries.[48] These enable us to traverse the path gradually. The extraordinary preliminaries[49] enable us—through their blessing, merit, and purification of negativities—to develop a special meditative concentration which we are then able to apply in practice. The meditation on the body of a yidam deity in the creation-stage and perfection-stage practices induces the realization of the true nature, exactly as it is.[50] Thus there are manifold different paths in putting the dharma into practice. All generate the energy potential of the result—namely, the realization of the primordial awareness of the dharmadhatu.

The Primordial Awarenesses and the Four Bodies of a Buddha

While performing the enlightened activity of a Buddha, the four kinds of primordial awareness in general possess the nature of the three bodies of a Buddha (Skt. *trikaya*). The mirrorlike primordial awareness knows everything, that is, both the true nature of dharmata which constitutes the absolute truth, as well as the appearances of phenomena[51] which constitute the relative truth. Due to this quality the mirrorlike primordial awareness corresponds to the 'body of a Buddha's qualities' (Skt. *dharmakaya*) which is also designated as the 'body of qualities for one's own benefit'. Since it possesses the qualities of excellent abandonment and excellent realization, excellent knowledge, excellent love, and excellent power of mind, and since it is free from all faults, it is designated as the body of a Buddha's qualities.

Although the Buddhas are endowed with all the qualities of knowledge, love, and power of mind, they cannot teach the mere, pure essence of mind and of primordial awareness to those to be trained, since this particular body has no form. The body of a Buddha's qualities merely comprises the qualities; it is not a body of form.

To be able to perform activities for the benefit of others a Buddha needs a concrete, manifest form. To create a mutual connection, no matter whether those to be trained are of pure or of impure karma, a Buddha needs a manifest body. It is not possible to create a connection solely through the mere knowledge and the mere love of the body of qualities. Such a manifest body of a Buddha is called a 'form body' (Skt. *rupakaya*). There are two kinds of form body: the body of perfect enjoyment (Skt. *sambhogakaya*) and the highest emanation body (Skt. *nirmanakaya*).

The body of perfect enjoyment is able to perform any kind of dharma activity. It is called the body of 'enjoyment' because it 'enjoys' the dharma. It is 'perfect' because it can perform any activity without exception in a perfect way. However, it only manifests itself to those with pure karma— those bodhisattvas dwelling on the bodhisattva levels. It is just from their perspective that the body of perfect enjoyment appears. Those needing to be trained who have impure karma cannot meet this body.

The essence of the body of perfect enjoyment is the primordial awareness of equality that views everything as equal, and the discriminating primordial awareness that knows every phenomenon specifically. This form body dwells in the pure realms and teaches those who actually dwell on the bodhisattva levels, not requiring tuition by means of speeches or lectures. Instead, while the Buddhas have perfect insight into the true nature of all phenomena, their enlightened activity radiates directly into the minds of those with such karmic good fortune. This way of teaching is called the 'knowledge transmission of the victorious ones'. Whatever appears in the enlightened mind of the Buddhas spontaneously appears to the students, who immediately understand it. In this way language is not needed.

Another way for the body of perfect enjoyment to teach is called the 'symbol transmission of the awareness holders'. It teaches those bodhisattvas who are not able to directly understand the Buddha's mind. Through the mere showing of a symbol they understand the enlightened intention. In these two ways the enjoyment body teaches the high bodhisattvas without the primordial awareness that accomplishes all actions. It only teaches by means of the primordial awareness of equality and the discriminating primordial awareness, because those to be trained are directly penetrated by the enlightened activity.

The third body of a Buddha is the highest emanation body. It is also a form body, it is an actual physical body, like that possessed by our teacher, Buddha Shakyamuni. He came to this earth in this kind of body, taught the dharma, and brought those to be tamed onto the path of liberation and omniscience. The highest emanation body possesses the essence of the primordial awareness that accomplishes all actions and is therefore also able to teach beings with pure karma. It does so by teaching those who dwell on the bodhisattva levels in that very form. Principally, however, it teaches the dharma to students with impure karma by using speech. It uses many different methods to teach all those to be trained. Because some of them do not yet have the karmic good fortune to enter the path of the true dharma, in those it sows the seed of liberation. For those who do have the good fortune to enter the path, but are not able to practice the dharma, it offers specific methods. The same is true for those who are indeed able to practice the true dharma, and for those with the karmic good fortune to attain the ultimate fruit through much sustained practice. According to the different capacities of the beings its enlightened activity is shown. In this way the highest emanation body works for the benefit of beings by means of the primordial awareness that accomplishes all actions.

In this way four of the five kinds of primordial awareness are connected with the three bodies of a Buddha. The fifth, the primordial awareness of the dharmadhatu, is not a phenomenon of the unadulterated realization of the way things appear, but is actually the true nature itself, just as it is—namely, emptiness. It can appear as a mirrorlike form because the essence of such a form—which is naturally empty and primordially nonexistent—is inseparable from the dharmadhatu. Equality is also included because it sees things as being equal. It includes the discriminating primordial awareness because it can also make distinctions. In addition, it includes the primordial awareness that accomplishes all actions because it is also connected to one's actions. Absolutely seeing, the dharmadhatu is free from all mental projections—its very nature is emptiness itself.

Our mind, however—as the eight collections of consciousness—grasps at the appearing aspect of everything,
taking it to be truly existent, and thus develops a tendency
towards strong dualistic grasping. When this dualistic
grasping is completely purified one sees all phenomena free
from projections, and thus comes to experience the true
nature, emptiness. Thus, it is true for all consciousnesses—
the all-base, the all-base consciousness, the klesha-mind, and
the six collections of consciousness—that, when their dualistic grasping is completely purified, the primordial awareness of the dharmadhatu is attained. It is the essence of all
the eight collections. The purified clarity aspect of the consciousnesses expresses itself in the first four kinds of primordial awareness, whereas the purified emptiness aspect
expresses itself in the primordial awareness of the dharmadhatu, which sees the emptiness of all phenomena.

The primordial awareness of the dharmadhatu pervades
all three bodies of a Buddha, because the body of qualities
is by its nature empty, as are the body of perfect enjoyment
and the highest emanation body. Therefore, the essence of
the primordial awareness of the dharmadhatu is called the
'essence body' (Skt. *svabhavikakaya*). It is the essence of all
phenomena, the naturally abiding emptiness.

Chapter Six
MEDITATION TO DEVELOP PRIMORDIAL AWARENESS

Although there are four causes for attaining primordial awareness,[52] of these, only the cause for the primordial awareness of equality requires meditation. This awareness encompasses the mind-training[53] through which a positive mental attitude, the 'enlightened attitude' (Skt. *bodhichitta*), is developed. In this, one meditates on loving-kindness and compassion in order to be able to ultimately benefit others.

One uses meditation methods mainly in order to give rise to the primordial awareness of the dharmadhatu in one's mind-stream. For those new to meditation the primordial awareness of the dharmadhatu does not arise in their mind-streams from the very beginning; therefore, there are different kinds of methods to enable it to arise and develop gradually.

According to the enlightened intention of the scriptures of the Middle Way philosophy (Skt. *madhyamaka*), one approaches the dharmadhatu by means of logical investigation and analysis. Appearances are analyzed until the realization arises that they do not truly exist from their own side and by means of their own essence. All phenomena are empty. No phenomenon has a self. When this realization arises in one's own mind-stream one then has to familiarize oneself with it thoroughly. This meditation is based on inference and is also designated as 'using inference as the path'.

The uncommon methods of the great seal (Skt. *mahamudra*) and the great perfection (Skt. *mahasandhi*) are meditations directly based on the essence of mind. One looks straight at one's own mind—that is, the consciousnesses— and its essence. It seems as if the mind is really there as an entity; therefore, one looks for its location and then analyzes its essence. This does not happen through inference but through direct investigation within one's own mindstream. We realize that the essence of mind is not present naturally, and this is exactly what is designated as emptiness, or the dharmadhatu.

There are two appropriate methods of mahamudra meditation to give rise to the primordial awareness of the dharmadhatu: looking while the mind is resting and looking while the mind is moving. The approach to the first method is the meditation of calm abiding. One lets one's mind rest until it abides calmly, and then with precision one looks at it. One looks for how it rests, for where it abides, and whoever or whatever it is that abides there. This is looking at the true nature of the mind while the mind is resting.

In order to look while the mind is moving, the mind needs to be in motion. In the meditation practice of calm abiding it also happens that the mind is moved by thoughts. Exactly at that moment, when the mind is actually in motion, one looks at it. One watches for what it is that moves, where the thoughts come from, where they abide, and where they go. This is not a way of looking that involves inference, but it is a way of looking straight at one's mind. In this way one comes to understand that the movements of mind are also naturally empty in the same way as the resting mind is naturally empty in its essence. One sees this emptiness directly. More detailed instructions on these kinds of meditation can be found in Karmapa Wangchug Dorje's *Ocean of Certainty* and *Pointing Out the Dharmakaya*. They offer methods for the gradual introduction into the essence of the primordial awareness of the dharmadhatu.

There are two causes that allow the primordial awareness of the dharmadhatu to arise in one's mind-stream: the direct cause, and the indirect cause. The direct cause is the straight-looking meditation on the true nature which is found in both calm abiding and deep insight meditations.

The indirect cause consists of purifying negativity and increasing experiences and realizations. Through the meditation practices of the preliminaries one accumulates merit as, for example, through the practices of prostrating, confessing negativities, or meditating on Vajrasattva. In this way one's own mind-stream is gradually purified and experiences and realizations increase. Trust and conviction in the dharma grow, and one's effort also increases through which, in turn, one's dharma practice intensifies. In addition, the creation-stage practice of a yidam deity contributes to the indirect cause, because it is also a useful method to give rise to experiences and realization within one's mind-stream.

When the primordial awareness of the dharmadhatu reveals itself more and more in this way, the other four primordial awarenesses will naturally arise as well. Due to the increase of the clarity aspect of the primordial awareness of the dharmadhatu they arise automatically in one's mind-stream.

Chapter Seven
THE FIVE BUDDHA-FAMILIES

Whoever allows the five kinds of primordial awareness to reveal themselves through meditation attains thereby the ultimate fruit; that is, the level of the five buddha-families. The lords of the five families—Vairochana, Akshobhya, Ratnasambhava, Amitabha, and Amoghasiddhi—are, in their essence, the five primordial awarenesses and duly appear in the form of the body of perfect enjoyment (Skt. *sambhogakaya*).

By purifying all of the consciousnesses you also purify the five mental afflictions (Skt. *klesha*), and thus the five kinds of primordial awareness gradually reveal themselves.

As for the primordial awareness of the dharmadhatu, it is the perfect transformation of the all-base consciousness and reveals itself when all ignorance and mental dullness—that is, the obscurations of mental afflictions and those impeding knowledge—are completely purified. It manifests as Vairochana, the lord of the 'Buddha' family,[54] the first of the five buddha-families. Vairochana (Tib. *rnam par snang mdzad*) means the 'One Who Completely Manifests'. He is the one who allows the true nature of phenomena to appear non-mistakenly and perfectly. He clarifies the nature of all phenomenal reality.

Akshobhya, the lord of the 'Vajra' family, is in essence the mirrorlike primordial awareness which reveals itself by means of the transformation of the all-base. In general, the

true nature, the essence of all phenomena, is natural emptiness. However, relative appearances arise that are dependent
on each other and are connected with one another. These
appear just like reflections in a mirror. Since these are seen
without any attachment or grasping whatsoever, he is called
Akshobhya (Tib. *mi bskyod pa*), the 'Unshakeable One'.
Through the transformation of the all-base the affliction of
anger is completely and perfectly purified. Considering all
mental afflictions, it is mainly anger that surges up in our
mind and makes it restless; therefore, the manifestation of
completely purified[55] anger is the 'Unshakeable One',
Akshobhya.

The third of the five lords of the buddha-families is Ratnasambhava. He is the lord of the 'Ratna'[56] family. His nature
is merit, wealth, and excellence, and therefore he is called
Ratnasambhava (Tib. *rin chen 'byung gnas*), the 'Source of
Preciousness'. He embodies the transformation of the
klesha-mind and thus the primordial awareness of equality. The nature of the klesha-mind is to grasp on to a self, a
pride that takes the self to be the highest and the best. When
the klesha-mind is abandoned, the pride accompanying that
high esteem of the self vanishes all by itself, under its own
power. Whoever develops pride closes the doors to all positive qualities. If you think you are the best, the most superior, you will not develop any new qualities. It is even said,
"To the ball of pride there is no possibility for any good qualities to stick." In this adage a proud person is compared to a
round ball. If someone were to pour water over it, not a single
drop would stick. Through the purification of pride, however, the foundation for all emerging merit, possessions, and
positive qualities is laid bare. For this reason the manifestation of the primordial awareness of equality and of perfectly
purified pride is the 'Source of Preciousness', Ratnasambhava.

Amitabha, the lord of the fourth buddha-family, the 'Lotus' family, is, in his essence, the discriminating primordial
awareness which reveals itself through the transformation

of the sixth consciousness, the mind consciousness, and through the perfect purification of desirous attachment. On the basis of the mind consciousness there arise desire, attachment, and grasping, due to which the true nature of all phenomena cannot be realized. It cannot be seen clearly, because the essence of desirous attachment is infatuation. Through perfect purification desirous attachment transforms into clarity, into the clear light of Amitabha, the Buddha of 'Infinite Light' (Tib. *'od dpag med*). His essence is freedom from attachment and the endowment of the most excellent highest understanding (Skt. *prajña*).

The fifth lord of the five buddha-families is Amoghasiddhi, the lord of the 'Karma' family. He embodies the revelation of the primordial awareness that accomplishes all actions, which is attained through the transformation of the five sense consciousnesses and the perfect purification of the affliction of jealousy. The essence of jealousy is contrary to the accomplishment of benefit. A jealous person is naturally one not able to perform actions for the benefit of others. If, however, the jealousy is pacified, the primordial awareness that accomplishes all actions is perfected. Through this awareness all actions and enlightened activities can be performed exactly in the right way and without hindrance. Due to this activity Amoghasiddhi (Tib. *don yod grub pa*) is the 'One Who Accomplishes What Is Meaningful'. Since it is his nature to accomplish the benefit of all sentient beings, the fifth lord of the five buddha-families embodies the primordial awareness that accomplishes all actions.

THE BUDDHAS AND THE FOUR KINDS OF ENLIGHTENED ACTIVITY

Each of the lords of the five buddha-families individually carries out one of the four kinds of enlightened activity. These are pacifying, increasing, empowering and wrathful enlightened activity.

Buddha Akshobhya represents the pacifying enlightened activity and grants the pacifying extraordinary achievements (Skt. *siddhi*). This enlightened activity is designated 'pacifying' because it pacifies sicknesses, spirits, hindrances, and all kinds of negative conditions. The mental afflictions are pacified by meditating on Akshobhya as a yidam deity, and thus also hindrances and negative conditions. How is it possible that through such enlightened activity sicknesses, hindrances and so forth can be pacified and that the pacifying extraordinary achievements are granted? Akshobhya is the self-expression of completely purified anger. Whoever is angry cannot find peace. Instead, all hindrances and negative conditions arise in him or her. The complete purification of anger by means of the practice of Akshobhya, aspirational prayers directed to him, or the meditation upon him allows the pacifying enlightened activity and the pacifying extraordinary achievements to arise.

The second type of enlightened activity, the increasing activity, is embodied by Ratnasambhava. 'Increasing' means to extend or increase life, merit, primordial awareness, or possessions. Due to pride, no positive qualities can be gained, merit cannot grow, and wealth cannot increase. Instead, these only diminish. The essence of completely purified pride, however, is Ratnasambhava, which is why the increasing enlightened activity will be effective when one visualizes him, meditates on him, prays to him, or applies his practice.

Completely pure desirous attachment expresses itself through Buddha Amitabha. A person guided by desire, attachment, or grasping becomes diffused and loses power over phenomena. Through completely purified desirous attachment, however, one is able to gain control over, and to independently coordinate, everything. This is because the entourage, possessions, merit, and so forth are controlled by the power of this Buddha. In this way Amitabha grants us the empowering enlightened activity and the empowering extraordinary achievements.

Amoghasiddhi is the self-expression of pure jealousy, upon which the wrathful enlightened activity is based. 'Wrathful' is used to designate the destruction of hindrances and negative conditions. Generally, due to the affliction of jealousy, we are not able to dissolve hindrances and negative conditions. On the contrary, our capabilities diminish. However, when jealousy is completely purified, we are able to destroy hindrances and negative conditions. For this reason, it is Amoghasiddhi who grants us the wrathful enlightened activity and the wrathful extraordinary achievements.

In the same order the above-mentioned four kinds of enlightened activities correspond to the mirrorlike primordial awareness, the primordial awareness of equality, the discriminating primordial awareness, and the primordial awareness that accomplishes all activities. The primordial awareness of the dharmadhatu, however, is the root of all these four kinds of primordial awareness. Therefore, Vairochana is the Buddha who gives rise to all of the four kinds of enlightened activity. He serves as the basis or origin for all the four kinds of enlightened activity, for all of the extraordinary achievements, and for all of the five buddha-families.

THE MEANING OF THE HAND-HELD SYMBOLS

Each of the five Buddhas holds a specific symbolic attribute: Vairochana holds a wheel, Akshobhya, a vajra, Ratnasambhava, a jewel; Amitabha, a lotus flower; and Amoghasiddhi, a double vajra. These symbols all have a specific meaning. Reflecting upon their meaning strengthens the actual meditation, serves to increase and stabilize the realization of the true nature of phenomena, and also helps to attain primordial awareness. For this reason I am going to explain the specific symbolic attributes of the five lords of the buddha-families.

The wheel held by Vairochana is a symbol for the authentic teachings (Skt. *dharma*). You also find it in other fields of Buddhism: it is, for example, always found above the entrances of Buddhist temples. Generally, a wheel is an object that turns and makes it possible for us to comfortably reach a certain destination. The wheel of the authentic teachings has eight spokes as a sign that it is possible to reach the ultimate destination of buddhahood by means of the eightfold path of the noble ones. Moreover, by means of the eightfold path of the noble ones it is possible to attain the primordial awareness of the dharmadhatu, which is the essence of Vairochana. As a representation of his essence, Vairochana holds the wheel of the authentic teachings.

Akshobhya holds the symbolic attribute of a vajra. He is the 'Unshakeable One', because his nature, completely pure anger, expresses itself in the form of patience and stability as well as the enlightened activity of pacifying. These are exactly what a vajra symbolizes. A vajra is the symbol for unchangeability and represents the endowment of a clear and stable way of appearing. In this way the vajra is the manifestation of the nature of Akshobhya.

Ratnasambhava holds a jewel as a symbol of his nature. Precious stones and jewels often represent the possession of perfect wealth, which is why the jewel is used as an example for the arising of happiness and joy. Ratnasambhava represents the enlightened activity of increase, multiplication, and the extension of life, merit, wealth, happiness, and joy. He is the expression of completely pure pride; therefore, he holds a jewel in his hand.

Amitabha is the lord of the fourth buddha-family. As a symbol of his nature he holds a lotus flower, which represents completely pure desirous attachment. When desirous attachment is perfectly purified, it resembles an utterly beautiful and attractive flower with bright colors and a perfect shape. A real flower of such beauty, however, is not an actual object for attachment and grasping because it is impermanent and its beauty ephemeral. One cannot keep its beauty as a possession for some hundreds of years. Because of impermanence and the flux of change, a flower is not a suitable object for which to develop attachment. When desirous attachment is completely purified, no attachment or grasping can arise in the least, no matter which object is involved. Since completely pure desirous attachment expresses itself through Buddha Amitabha, he holds a lotus flower in his hand.

The symbol for Amoghasiddhi is the double vajra. As explained above, a vajra symbolizes unchangeability. Generally, where there is no change there is no way anything can progress to a more superior state of being. Something that is unchangeable cannot degenerate and turn towards faults, nor can it increase positive qualities. As a sign that it is nevertheless possible to increase qualities through which meaningful activity for the benefit of beings can be performed, Amoghasiddhi, the 'One Who Accomplishes What Is Meaningful', holds a double vajra in his hand.

THE APPEARANCES OF THE BUDDHAS IN THE INTERMEDIATE PHASE OF THE BARDO

The five kinds of primordial awareness demonstrate the perspective of a Buddha's quality body (Skt. *dharmakaya*). In our present impure situation these are obscured by the eight collections of consciousness, because of our ignorance and our delusion about their appearances. Though the primordial awarenesses are obscured, they are still actually present within ourselves. Even though they are obscured now, this does not alter their essence. They are naturally present within the mind-stream of all sentient beings. The presence of the five kinds of primordial awareness is, from the point of view of the Yogachara-madhyamaka philosophy (Shentong),[57] also called the 'potential', the 'element', or the 'heart-essence of those gone to bliss' (Skt. *sugatagarbha*).[58]

This designates what is also called the 'buddha-nature'. Since its self-nature is the five kinds of primordial awareness, it is naturally present within the mind-stream of each sentient being. In order to reveal the buddha-nature one has to liberate oneself from all ignorance and delusion concerning the appearances of the eight collections of consciousness. This revelation is also called the 'attainment of a Buddha's quality body'.

A sign indicating the presence of the five kinds of primordial awareness within all sentient beings is their appearance in the form of the lords of the five buddha-families. The way they manifest their appearance is described in the well-known book *Liberation through Hearing in the Bardo* (also known as the "Tibetan Book of the Dead"). Because of the inherent self-nature of the five primordial awarenesses, the five Buddhas naturally appear when the appearances of the intermediate phase of the bardo manifest. But how is it possible that they can take on an appearance in this way?

As long as we are alive there is a connection between our body and our mind. For as long as our mind is present within our body, the flesh of our body does not decay, and the bones will not reveal themselves as our skeleton. But the mind is bound to the body. It cannot wander around freely without limit as the bardo consciousness does, but is permanently with the body. This is the sign of the connection between body and mind. This connection is kept intact by the so-called royal life-force. This is the life energy that moves for as long as we live between the white aspect which is present at the top of our head and the red aspect which is present at the lower part of the body.[59] The mind coheres with this energy of the royal life-force and is in this way bound by it.

During the process of dying the royal life-force dissolves. The function of this force was to keep the red and the white aspects apart. Now, the connection of body and mind collapses and due to the lack of power of the life-force, the white aspect that used to be present above it sinks down, while the red aspect that used to be present below it moves up. The moment these two meet at the level of the heart the separation of the mind from the body takes place. This causes the dissolution of the body sensations right up till the last movement of breath. Gradually the body sensations disappear—those that are based on the earth element, the water element, the fire element, and the air element, each one after the other. Thereafter, the inner thoughts of the mind are interrupted—those thoughts that arise due to desirous attachment, due to anger, and due to dullness. These thoughts are also called the 'eighty natural thoughts'.[60] After this dissolution the different appearances of the bardo manifest. From the aspect of complete purity there are three different kinds of bardo: the dharmakaya bardo, the sambhogakaya bardo, and the nirmanakaya bardo.

Within the process of dying the dharmakaya bardo appears first. As was already explained, the essence of the primordial awareness of the dharmadhatu is emptiness without a focus. After the collapse of the eighty natural thoughts precisely this essence appears to us in the form of emptiness. When one has trained well in meditative concentration during one's lifetime, it is possible that when the emptiness appears, then the 'mother clear light unites with the child clear light'. The 'mother clear light' is the designation for the appearance of emptiness at this point, whereas the 'child clear light' designates one's own meditation practice of emptiness that one trained in while one was alive. If these two are unified at this moment, the true nature of phenomena will reveal itself. If, however, one did not gain much meditation experience, the appearance of emptiness after the collapse of the natural thoughts will still appear, but one will not recognize the true nature in it. Instead, it seems as if one was falling unconscious, so that the function of one's mind was automatically stopped. However, one will emerge again from this phase.

This phase in which the true nature shines forth is designated the dharmakaya bardo.[60] Some practitioners are interested in the duration of these intermediate phases. The number of days one spends in either of the three types of bardo is determined by one's meditative concentration and mental stability. The length of the period one is able to spend in meditation within the true nature when it appears at this point is counted in 'days of mental stability'. These are dependent on the capacity of one's present meditation practice; that is, for how long one is able to abide in meditative equipoise while still alive. It depends on the duration of one's abiding in uncontrived meditative concentration right now. If, for example, a person is able to meditate for one minute within uncontrived meditative concentration while alive, his or her mental stability in the phase of the dharmakaya bardo will continue for five minutes. If this person is able to abide in such a meditation for one hour while still alive, the mental stability of the dharmakaya bardo will last for five hours.[62] The duration of this phase of abiding is only dependant on one's meditation practice; no other conditions influence it. This means that if one trains in meditation practice very well, the phases of the different kinds of bardo can appear much longer. If one did not practice at all, one's mind will not be able to rest for long, but will change from moment to moment. And one will not be able to consciously recognize the true nature; therefore, it will appear for only a short while.

When one emerges again from the dharmakaya bardo, the sambhogakaya bardo will appear. Since the five kinds of primordial awareness are present in our mind-stream as its self-nature while still alive, and since these can appear in the form of the lords of the five buddha-families, they will now appear one after the other in the sambhogakaya bardo.

First of all, the manifestation of the Buddha Vairochana will appear. He is seated on a throne that is supported by eight lions. Vairochana's body is white in color. He holds his hands in the gesture of teaching the dharma, which is symbolized by a wheel. His legs are in the full vajra posture. He is adorned with all of the sambhogakaya ornaments.[63] How is it possible that he appears exactly in this way? It is the primordial awareness contained in our mind that takes form in this manifestation. Its energy potential shines forth in the sambhogakaya bardo as the Buddha Vairochana in the midst of a manifestation of white light. When he appears, we should be able to recognize him as a Buddha.[64]

If we do not recognize him, the Buddha Akshobhya will then appear. He is seated on a throne supported by eight elephants. His body color is blue. His right hand is held in the earth-touching gesture and his left in the gesture of meditation. His legs are in the full vajra position. He is adorned with all of the sambhogakaya ornaments. The reason for his appearing in this form is the mirrorlike primordial awareness that is present in our mind. The manifestation of Akshobhya's body form is the innate indication that the mirrorlike primordial awareness is present in one's mind.

After that, Buddha Ratnasambhava will appear. He is seated on a throne supported by eight horses. His body color is yellow. He holds his right hand in the gesture of supreme generosity and his left in the gesture of meditation. His legs are in the full vajra posture. He is adorned with all of the sambhogakaya ornaments. Since one's own impure thoughts are interrupted in the process of dying, this makes it possible for the primordial awareness of equality to manifest itself here in the sambhogakaya bardo. Its particular way of appearing is as the body form of Buddha Ratnasambhava.

Then Buddha Amitabha appears. He is seated on a throne supported by eight peacocks. He holds both his hands in the gesture of meditation. His legs are in the full vajra posture. He is adorned with all of the sambhogakaya ornaments.

He is the self-expression of the discriminating primordial awareness which is continuously present in our mind-stream and which appears in the sambhogakaya bardo as the manifestation of the body form of Buddha Amitabha.

The self-expression of the primordial awareness that accomplishes all activities is Buddha Amoghasiddhi. He is seated on a throne supported by eight *shangshang* birds.[65] His body color is green. His right hand is held in the gesture of granting protection and his left in the gesture of meditation. His legs are in the full vajra posture. He is adorned with all of the sambhogakaya ornaments. In this way the primordial awareness that accomplishes all activities embodies itself in the appearance of Buddha Amoghasiddhi in the sambhogakaya bardo.

In this phase of the sambhogakaya bardo, many other deities appear after the lords of the five buddha-families. They are all described in the "Tibetan Book of the Dead," *Liberation through Hearing in the Bardo.* These deities represent the pure fifty-one mental formations.[66] Since the topic here concerns the five kinds of primordial awareness connected to the five buddha-families, but not generally the bardo per se, I will not describe the way of appearing of all these deities.

Some people doubt that the lords of the five buddha-families indeed appear as herein described. They believe they may be dressed differently or that they may appear in a different manifestation if there is a different situation. Even some Tibetan scholars think like this. The Tibetan scholar Gendün Chöpel from Amdo, for example, mentioned in this context: "We meditate on the deities following the tradition of the Indians. If we were following the tradition of the Chinese, the deities would all be sporting a wispy Chinese moustache!" In reality this is not true. The way the five Buddhas appear does not originate from either the Indian tradition or from the Tibetan. It was described by the Buddha

Shakyamuni in person in the tantras. The exact description can be found in the Kangyur.[67] The deities are not the Buddha's invention either; they are actually present within our mind. They are there like a seed within the energy-channels (Skt. *nadi*) of our body, and can therefore appear in the intermediate phase of the bardo. One may also manifest them while still alive; through certain kinds of meditation methods, one actually comes to see them. These deities appear to the practitioners who, for example, intensely train in the method of *thögal*[68]; thus they may be perceived directly during one's lifetime. The external appearance of the deities through that specific practice is a sign that they are actually present internally, inside our body. By no stretch of the imagination are they free fantasy!

The nirmanakaya bardo corresponds to what is usually called the 'bardo of becoming'.[69] In this phase one prepares oneself for taking on a new corporeal form. On the basis of the nirmanakaya's enlightened activity it is possible to enter a new life.

Generally speaking, it is very important to train in meditative concentration and to meditate on the essence of the primordial awarenesses. The knowledge of the defining characteristics, the divisions, and the nature of the five kinds of primordial awareness enhances and increases meditative concentration at any time. This knowledge is especially important for the appearances of the bardo because, if the respective Buddhas are recognized as such, one can attain buddhahood in the sambhogakaya bardo. In addition, the lords of the five buddha-families are very important for the attainment of the ultimate aim. For this reason meditation is done on their form bodies in the practice of the creation phase. For those who do not train in this specific creation phase practice as well, it is important and beneficial to know what the actual nature of a Buddhist deity is, for it proves the necessity of meditation.

THE TRANSFORMATION OF THE FIVE ELEMENTS INTO THE FEMALE BUDDHAS

The practice of Secret Mantrayana emphasizes the union of method and wisdom. Method is symbolized by the five male Buddhas, and wisdom by the five female Buddhas. At the level of complete purity, the five lords of the buddha-families are, as we know already, the expression of the pure afflictions. Similarly, the five female wisdom-manifestations are the pure elements.

In general, the basis for worldly appearances appearing to sentient beings are the five elements of earth, water, fire, wind, and space. All outer objects arise due to having the elements as their constituents. What, then, do the five elements represent or symbolize, in terms of their function?

The lord of the first buddha-family is Akshobhya, the expression of completely pure anger. His consort is called Mamaki, who is the expression of the completely pure element of water. In its negative manifestation, anger can cause both harm and destruction. However, in anger there is also a certain positive potentiality that can give rise to positive results. Similarly, the element of water has two aspects. If water appears to us in a haphazard and dangerous way, it can cause much harm and destruction. However, since it has the qualities of being both fluid and adhesive, water benefits through cohesion. Were even the tiniest particle to entirely lack the element of water, desiccated and dust-like it would soon fall apart and scatter. When the element of water is present, the constituent parts cannot scatter, but are held together in perfect cohesion. In this way Mamaki expresses the completely pure element of water.

Ratnasambhava is the expression of completely pure pride. His consort, Buddhalochana, is the completely pure element of earth. In general, earth is solid, hard, and unmoving. Even so, it is the ground from which everything grows and develops. The element of earth provides the creative potentiality for everything to grow and for everything to abide. Admittedly, earth can also wreak havoc, but in general everything depends on this element for its quality of abiding. There is also a negative aspect of pride: when it is empowered by afflictions, it then naturally constitutes the root for harmful actions to come about. When pride, however, assumes an aspect of courage, it can also give rise to positive qualities, such as determination in the conviction of thinking, "I am able to accomplish this." In this way pride becomes a source of stability much like the element earth. The ground provides a stable base upon which we can stand. Since earth has this nature of stability, the completely pure element of earth is expressed in Buddhalochana.

The completely pure affliction of desirous attachment is expressed by Amitabha. His consort, Pandaravasini, is the pure element of fire. Fire has the qualities of being both hot and burning. The fact that fire burns may cause a great deal of harm; on the other hand, heat is beneficial in that it causes ripening. Heat pervades everywhere, and lets fruit and crops ripen fully. No matter what the phenomenon, the root for its ripening is the element of fire. The affliction of attachment is said to burn in that it arouses the manifold sufferings of existence. In its positive aspect, however, just as heat has the power to ripen, attachment has the power to control. Thus Pandaravasini is said to be the expression of the completely pure element of fire.

The fourth wisdom-manifestation is Samayatara, the completely pure element of wind. She is the consort of Amoghasiddhi, who embodies completely pure jealousy. Jealousy as a negative emotion needs to be abandoned, but its more positive aspect is to bestow courage and determination to accomplish all actions. How does the element of wind actually work? When wind is in turmoil, it can scatter and destroy. In its positive manifestation, however, wind develops and embraces all activities. Since wind is light and moving, it is the basis for any and all kinds of movement. A tree, for example, can develop and spread its leaves merely due to the element of wind. And any kind of action one wishes to undertake depends for its execution on the element of wind, because it provides the possibility of movement. Thus wind is the very essence of the enlightened activity that accomplishes all actions, and therefore the female wisdom-manifestation of Amoghasiddhi, the one who accomplishes what is meaningful, is Samayatara, the completely pure element of wind.

The fifth lord, Vairochana, expresses the primordial awareness of dharmadhatu, completely pure mental dullness, or ignorance. His consort is the completely pure element of space, Dhatvishvari. The entire worldly realm is predicated on space. Since space is naturally empty in essence, there is nothing present within it. Yet, based on this emptiness, it is possible that various phenomena can grow, increase, and spread. We can move wherever we want because of there being empty space to move into. Trees, crops, and all other kinds of plants can grow only within empty space. All of the activities of the world are possible only because of the non-obstructive openness of space. Space allows all kinds of movement to take place. If there were no space, all phenomena would be jumbled up together, and there would simply be no room to move or to breathe. All of this happens because of the non-obstructive openness of space. When one clears away the affliction of ignorance or mental dullness, the meaning of emptiness is realized. From the ultimate point of view one says: "Wherever there is emptiness, there is possibility; without emptiness nothing whatsoever is possible." Thus, since space offers the possibility for anything to happen, its pure aspect is expressed in the form of Dhatvishvari.

These five elements constitute the outer world and our own body as well. If the elements are in balance, everything runs smoothly without fuss or disturbance. Imbalance, however, produces problems.

When the energy of the elements constituting the physical body flows regularly and evenly, the body is stable and remains healthy. There is no prospect of sickness. However, when the five elements fall out of balance, when they are disturbed, or when their energy decreases, one feels weak and the body becomes sick. In this case, or, conversely, when one is feeling fine and wishes to prevent any future discomfort or sickness, the meditation and practice of the Medicine Buddha is recommended. It is even more effective if this meditation is conjoined with a special visualization on the five elements.

Chapter Eight
MEDITATION TO BALANCE THE ELEMENTS IN THE BODY

From the point of view of complete purity there are the five female wisdom-manifestations. From the point of view of the impure these appear in the form of the five elements. The physical body is naturally based on the elements: the flesh corresponds to the element of earth, the blood to water, the heat to fire, the breath to wind, and the consciousness to space. When the five elements in the body are stable, balanced, and settled, one feels happy and healthy. When they fall out of balance, one becomes sick and feels unwell. In order to keep a healthy balance of the five elements and thus to improve the strength of your flesh, blood, heat, breath, and consciousness, visualize your own body in the form of the Medicine Buddha and concentrate on the syllable *HUNG* in your heart-center.

First of all, from this syllable, the expression of the element of fire radiates in the form of red light pervading the entire outer world. Extracting the essence of the fire element from this environment, the red light increases in radiance and expands. The light enters your body through the heart-center and melts into the syllable *HUNG*, suffusing it completely with the energy of the fire element, which then burns all indispositions and sickly tendencies of the body, thus restoring it to the well-balanced state of good health.

Thereafter, the expression of the element of earth radiates in the form of yellow light from the syllable *HUNG*. It totally pervades the world, encompassing all that is of the nature of earth, such as hills, mountains, and islands. Having extracted the energy of the earth element from all worldly phenomena, the brilliantly energized light melts back into the body, mainly into the flesh, through the seedsyllable *HUNG*. Thus the whole body is vibrating from the union of the energy of all external and internal earth elements.

Now white light radiates from the syllable *HUNG* and touches all that is of the nature of the water element, such as springs, rivers, and oceans. Their essence is extracted and absorbed into the white light, which now becomes extremely lustrous and irradiated. All of this white light melts into the body, nourishing the blood and causing your complexion to become smooth and healthy.

In one's body the breath is of the nature of the wind element. It accounts for all movement inside the body and moves in its own ways of its own accord. The wind of the life force is located in the central channel. When this kinglike wind of the life force abides steadily, you will be healthy and life is stable. Should it move incorrectly, however, you would feel uncomfortable, and were it to stop moving, you would die. When the life force is weak, the branch winds will be weak and sickly as well. In order to increase the healthy energy of the winds in the body, visualize green light radiating from the *HUNG* in your heart-center. This green light gathers together the energy of the wind element, becomes irradiated with brilliance and strength, and melts back into your body. It diffuses throughout the whole body and restores the energy of the wind element in all those areas where it is weak. In this way the entire body becomes vibrantly energized.

The fifth element is the element of space. In general, space is empty and provides openness. The element of space corresponds to the internal consciousness, which is naturally empty in essence just like space. Even so, this emptiness is not a fixed state, but is naturally clear. Should the energy of the space element lose its balance, the mind may become dull, depressed, or simply overtaken by thoughts. When one is depressed and miserable, one suffers and cannot find the energy to do the simplest thing. In order to strengthen the energy of the space element, visualize blue light radiating from the *HUNG*, extracting the essence of the element of space, which is the energy of emptiness that provides spacious openness. The light melts into the *HUNG* and likewise into the whole body. Based on the energy of the space element, the whole body and mind become brilliant and energized. This is the way to meditate in order to enhance the energy of the elements in your body.

In general, most non-Buddhist religions meditate on the deity as being outside the physical body. In these cases the deity takes the form of a refuge, or of a protector or messenger. Thus do they meditate, and of course this is fine. In the Buddhist tradition, however, the deity is not meditated on as being outside the physical body. One meditates on the deity as being one's own essence expressing itself through oneself arising as the deity. One therefore thinks, "I *am* the deity," and with this conviction one meditates. Why is it justifiable to meditate in this manner? As previously seen, the five afflictions are actually self-expressions of the five kinds of primordial awareness; thus our own mind is in essence exactly the same as the mind of a Buddha. In the philosophical treatises this is sometimes referred to as 'sugatagarbha' or 'buddha-nature'.

Because all beings possess this innately pure buddha-nature, they are pure by nature and not at all impure. Being pure by nature it is perfectly justified to meditate that you are the deity, because this is exactly how it is!

Thus thinking, "I am the Medicine-Buddha," and allowing the light to radiate from the seed-syllable *HUNG* in the heart-center, gathering together the energy of the elements and dissolving this energy back into yourself does actually benefit. Alternatively, should you wish to benefit others, dissolve this highly energized light into them instead of yourself. In this way one helps them rebalance their elements. Thus your practice becomes beneficially effective for yourself and for others.

Notes

1. The five aggregates (Skt. *skandha*) are what constitute a person: the form, sensations, discernment, formation, and consciousness.

The twelve sense sources (Skt. *ayatana*) are the six inner sense sources, i.e., the sense faculties—the eye, ear, nose, tongue, body, and mind consciousness, and the six outer sense sources, i.e., the sense objects—form, sound, smell, tastes, physically tangible objects, and phenomena.

The eighteen elements (Skt. *dhatu*) include in addition to the twelve sense sources the respective consciousnesses—the eye, ear, nose, tongue, body, and mind consciousnesses.

2. 'Absorbing consciousness' is another name for the all-base consciousness (Skt. *alayavijñana*), describing part of its function. The whole function of the all-base consciousness will be described later on in this book.

3. *len pa'i rnam par shes pa zab shing phra/ bdag tu rtog pa gyur na mi rung bshed*

4. See bibliography for information on these two titles. Jamgön Kongtrul Lodrö Thayé also explained the same topic in his *Treasury of Knowledge* (Tib. *Shes bya kun khyab mdzod*).

5. Definition of body: *bem po rdul du grub pa*—matter composed of atoms

6. Definition of mind: *gsal zhing rig pa*—clear and cognizing

7. This phase of conditioned existence is called 'impure', because karma and mental afflictions aren't yet purified. As a result a new body will be taken on, through which sentient beings again accumulate karma and mental afflictions.

8. As mentioned in the introduction, there are three types of highest understanding (Tib. *shes rab*): the highest understanding of listening, that of reflecting, and that of meditating.

9. According to Buddhist philosophy, desire, anger, and likewise all the mental afflictions (Skt. *klesha*) are nothing other than thoughts. All of the multicolored variety of emotions and feelings that are so important and highly regarded in Western culture do not belong to the categorization of feeling per se. There are just three kinds of feeling: pleasant, unpleasant, or neutral.

10. This and the following Tibetan descriptions of the faculties are quoted from Mipham Rinpoche's *mKhas 'jug (Gateway to Knowledge)*. *Mig gi dbang po zar ma'i me tog lta bu*: In most of the current translations *zar ma'i me tog* is translated as 'sesame flower'. According to Sangye Gyamtso in *Tibetan Medical Paintings, Illustrations to the Blue Beryl* (Harry N. Abrams, 1992), it designates a flax flower (Lat. *Linum ussitatissimum*). Daniel Winkler, expert in Tibetan botanical sciences and co-translator (into German) of the above book, also considers the flax flower more possible, because flax is widely cultivated in Tibet. During the time when it blooms, endless fields are illuminated by the color of its steel-blue blossoms. The Tibetans use the flax seed for linseed oil production.

11. *rNa'i dbang po dro ga'i 'dzer pa gcus pa lta bu*: Acharya Lama Tengyal describes *'dzer pa* as something similar to a wart growing in the bark of trees. During a walk with Lama Namse Rinpoche I pointed out the typical growths in the bark of birch trees and he called them also exactly *'dzer pa*.

12. *sNa'i dbang po zangs kyi mo khab gshibs pa lta bu*: *Mo khab* are extremely fine needles. According to Tenga Rinpoche, *mo* refers to the thickness of the needles. As Thrangu Rinpoche stresses next, *zangs* refers to the copper color of the needles.

13. *lCe'i dbang po zla ba bkas pa lta bu*: *Zla ba bkas pa* could either be singular or plural. Acharya Lama Tengyal describes two half-moons. This corresponds to what is taught in the *bsdus grwa* of the Gelug tradition. There it says that the tongue faculty is located on the upper part of the tongue and the two half-moons are just a hair's breadth apart from each other.

14. *Lus kyi dbang po bya reg na 'jam gyi pags pa lta bu*: Thrangu Rinpoche said, as is also said here in the *mKhas 'jug*, the 'skin' of the bird Regnajam (Soft to Touch). Elsewhere it is translated as the 'plumage' of this bird.

15. The problem here is that the actual perceiver is our mind, and mind is mental, not material.

16. Outer objects are the objects perceived by the sense consciousnesses; they are said to be 'outside' the mind. Inner objects are all mental objects such as thoughts, memories, and the respective consciousnesses of the outer objects.

17. Thrangu Rinpoche, Halscheid 1998: "This is due to the clarity aspect of mind which is never interrupted. Mind is, according to its definition, clear and cognizing. If the clarity aspect were interrupted, you would not be able to distinguish it from a stone. Even within thought-free meditation, while fainting, or in the process of being anaesthetized, the clarity aspect of mind continues to function in the form of the two stable kinds of consciousness."

18. *nyon mongs pa can gyi yid*—klesha-mind

19. I added this reason in order to aid better understanding. I took it from explanations in *The Ornament of Rangjung Dorje's Intention in His Commentary that Distinguishes between Consciousness and Primordial Awareness* by Jamgön Kongtrul Lodrö Thayé. Here he says:

> The klesha-mind as well dwells in the all-base and arises from it. It does not realize that one's mind in itself is free from stains, and instead focuses on the all-base which is the mind endowed with stains. It is accompanied by [a] the idea of an 'I', by [b] pride that is seizing through thinking "I am the best", by [c] attachment and longing that take the 'I' to be more important than 'other', and by [d] ignorance through not realizing the 'I' itself as false. It is permanently covered by these four mental afflictions. ... (p. 94)

20. The definition of principal mind is: the awareness of merely the object—*gtso sems yul tsam rig pa*. The definition of mental events is: the awareness of the objects' particular details—*sems byung yul gyi khyad par rig pa*.

21. 'View' is defined as highest understanding (Skt. *prajña*) endowed with mental afflictions. It thus includes a certain clarity aspect.

22. 'Noble one' (Skt. *arya*) designates a bodhisattva on one of the ten bodhisattva levels.

23. 'Hearer' (Skt. *shravaka*) designates a Buddhist of the lesser vehicle (Skt. *hinayana*) who aspires to overcome suffering through meditating on the non-existence of a self of the person. The nirvana of the shravakas is called 'arhatship'.

24. When virtue arises due to karma and mental afflictions, as is the case here due to grasping at a self, it is called 'defiled virtue'. This will lead in turn to more karma and mental afflictions.

25. As for the klesha-mind, Karmapa Rangjung Dorje stresses the explanation of this seventh consciousness much more than Mipham Rinpoche and thus divides it into two aspects: the 'immediate mind' and the 'klesha-mind'. According to Rangjung Dorje, the immediate mind is the condition for the arising as well as the ceasing of each moment of consciousness of any of the six collections of consciousness. Thus its function is to let the six consciousnesses arise and let them cease again. The second aspect of the seventh consciousness inflicts the mind with the pride of the conception of an 'I', and thus lets the mental afflictions arise. That is why this aspect is called the 'mind endowed with afflictions', i.e., klesha-mind.

26. In his introduction Rinpoche called the two aspects of the all-base consciousness: 'all-base' and 'all-base consciousness'. In terms of its being the storehouse for karmic imprints, the 'all-base that seizes karmic imprints' can also just be designated 'all-base'. In terms of its bringing forth appearances, i.e., the process of making them conscious, the 'all-base of complete ripening' is designated as a consciousness, namely the 'all-base consciousness'.

27. This means that mind, i.e., the all-base consciousness, appears in two aspects: as the object to be perceived (in this case the form) and as the perceiving consciousness (in this case the eye consciousness).

28. This is precisely the point at which the followers of the Chittamatra school doubt the existence of the outer world and even consider it unnecessary, inferring that the whole of outer reality is the same as the inner reality, i.e., mind only.

29. Since the mental events perceive the particular details of the objects, whereas the principal mind generally just notices that there *is* an object, one can say that mental events are the product of an even more intense clarity aspect of mind.

30. The five 'ever-present mental events' are attraction, sensation, perception, attention, and contact (Mipham Rinpoche's *Gateway to Knowledge*, Vol. 1, p. 23). The following lists of mental events are taken from the same source. The names of the main categories of the mental events I translated according to the current explanations of Thrangu Rinpoche, which is why they differ slightly.

31. The five 'mental events with certainty over the object' are intention, interest, recollection, concentration, and discrimination (ibid., p. 24).

32. The eleven 'virtuous mental events' are faith, conscientiousness, pliancy, equanimity, conscience, shame, non-attachment, non-aggression, non-delusion, non-violence, and diligence (ibid., pp. 24-25).

33. The six 'root afflictions' are ignorance, attachment, anger, arrogance, doubt, and belief (ibid., pp. 25-26). The twenty secondary afflictions are fury, resentment, spite, hostility, envy, hypocrisy, pretense, lack of conscience, shamelessness, concealment, stinginess, self-infatuation, lack of faith, laziness, heedlessness, forgetfulness, non-alertness, lethargy, excitement, and distraction (ibid., pp. 27-29).

34. The four 'variable mental events' are sleep, regret, conception, and discernment (ibid., pp. 29-30).

35. Thrangu Rinpoche, teaching about the bardo, Halscheid 1999: "Generally there are forty-two peaceful deities, eight awareness-holders (Skt. *vidyadhara*), and just fifty wrathful deities. In the case of their visualization within the brain, however, the second aspect of Buddha Heruka, i.e., his appearance as Chemchok Heruka, counts as well. Thus there are fifty-one wrathful deities corresponding to the fifty-one mental events."

36. *rnam rtog shas che na dbugs 'byin ngub la rten nas bsgom par bya/*

37. 'Setting the mind' is the first of nine stages of mind coming to rest. It is described in the *Treasury of Knowledge* by Jamgön Kongtrul Lodrö Thayé, in the chapter "The Stages of Meditation of Shamatha and Vipashyana": "Setting the mind: having withdrawn from outer objects, the mind is directed towards an inner object of observation" (translated by Kiki Ekselius and Chryssoula Zerbini, p. 22).

38. 'Continuous setting' is the second stage of mind coming to rest: "Continuous setting: having turned to the first object, the mind is able to remain continuously on it without being distracted elsewhere" (ibid., slightly altered translation).

39. 'Resetting' is the third stage of mind coming to rest: "Resetting: having become aware of distraction towards outer objects, the mind is set once again on its object of observation" (ibid.).

40. Creation-stage as well as completion-stage practice are parts of the deity visualization of the Vajrayana. Within the creation-stage

practice you visualize the deity, i.e., you 'create' it as a mental image, either of yourself transformed (self-visualization), or in front, as if objectively (in-front visualization).

41. The 'four causes for attaining primordial awareness' are listed in Jamgön Kongtrul Lodrö Thayé's *Ornament of Rangjung Dorje's Intention in His Commentary that Distinguishes between Consciousness and Primordial Awareness*, p. 104. This list of four I took from this source. Thrangu Rinpoche explains them in the following passage. In addition, Lodrö Thayé describes further 'four causes for the transformation into primordial awareness'. These, however, refer to the transformation as interpreted by Rangjung Dorje. For completeness and as a possibility for comparison I will mention these here, in the same way as Thrangu Rinpoche presented them in 1998 in Halscheid: The all-base is the cause for the transformation into the mirrorlike primordial awareness, the klesha-mind (as one part of the seventh consciousness) is the cause for the primordial awareness of equality, the immediate mind (the second part of the seventh consciousness) is the cause for the discriminating primordial awareness, and the six collections of consciousness are the cause for the primordial awareness that accomplishes all actions.

42. *Tripitaka: vinayapitaka, sutrapitaka* and *abhidharmapitaka*.

43. Definition of 'primordial awareness that knows the nature of reality exactly as it is': *dngos po'i gnas lugs phyin ci ma log par rtogs pa*—the unadulterated realization of the true nature of things.

44. Definition of 'primordial awareness that knows the nature of reality to its full extent': *dngos po'i snang tshul phyin ci ma log par rtogs pa*—the unadulterated realization of the way things appear.

45. In reply to my request to define the meaning of 'dharma' in the word 'dharmadhatu', Rinpoche described dharma as emptiness. He said, "Dharmadhatu is the expanse of emptiness, the dharma-expanse." When 'dharmadhatu' is translated as 'expanse of phenomena' in other contexts, this precisely refers to emptiness, because all phenomena are empty by their self-nature. The translation as 'expanse of qualities' emphasizes the simultaneously present quality that allows phenomena to appear, i.e., the clarity aspect. This is according to the interpretation of Maitreya's *Uttaratantrashastra* (The Highest Continuum). It also emphasizes a Buddha's qualities that arise from focusing on emptiness. This is according to the interpretation of Maitreya's *Madhyantavibhanga* (Distinguishing the Middle from the Extremes).

46. The delusion is to believe that they do indeed truly exist externally in the way they appear to exist, i.e., as concrete, independent forms.

47. In the teachings of the great seal (Skt. *mahamudra*) or the great perfection (Skt. *mahasandi*) it is said that due to strong clinging the mind gets lost in this overaccentuated clarity aspect.

48. The general preliminaries of mahamudra are the 'four thoughts that turn the mind': reflecting on the difficulty of obtaining a precious human body, reflecting on impermanence and death, reflecting on karmic actions and their results, and reflecting on the disadvantages of the cyclic existence of samsara.

49. The four extraordinary preliminaries are: taking refuge and developing the enlightened attitude while prostrating, purifying negativities through the practice of Vajrasattva, accumulating merit through the mandala-offering, and the transfer of blessing through the practice of guru-yoga.

50. Meditating on a yidam deity is a method to gradually develop the primordial awareness that knows the nature of reality exactly as it is, i.e., the unadulterated realization of the true nature of things.

51. Here Rinpoche uses the terms *chos nyid* and *chos can*. *Chos nyid* (Skt. *dharmata*) designates the true nature of phenomena, whereas *chos can* designates that which possesses the true nature of phenomena, that is, the phenomena themselves.

52. The four causes for attaining primordial awareness are (1) the highest understanding of listening as the cause for the mirrorlike primordial awareness, (2) meditation on equality as the cause for the primordial awareness of equality, (3) teaching the dharma to others as the cause for the discriminating primordial awareness, and (4) performing actions for the benefit of others as the cause for the primordial awareness that accomplishes all actions. See above, chapter 5.

53. 'Mind-training' (*lojong*) refers to the 'Seven Points of Mind-Training' taught by Chekawa Yeshe Dorje, a twelfth-century master of the Kadampa lineage of Tibetan Buddhism.

54. Within the five buddha-families, the first is called the 'Buddha' family. In order to indicate the difference between these two, the first part of all of the particular names of the specific buddha-families has been printed in simple quotes.

55. Rinpoche mentions again and again that the specific mental affliction is purified, and that the Buddhas are the manifestation of the completely pure affliction. 'Purification' in this context, however, has no dualistic meaning, such as there being mental afflictions of which the mind must be purified, and finally these are no longer present because they have been transformed into primordial awareness. The same is valid for 'transformation'—it does not mean that there is, say, one thing in the beginning, namely the affliction or the consciousness, which afterwards changes into another thing, namely primordial awareness. According to the intention of all the madhyamaka schools, the ordinary mind including the afflictions is nothing other than illusion-like delusion. We merely think that these truly exist. This assumption that phenomena, mind, and the self exist truly must be abandoned, and only then can we see their actual nature. Within the meaning of the Yogachara-madhyamaka philosophy (Shentong), the actual nature of the afflictions is primordial awareness from the very beginning, and the actual nature of mind is primordial awareness as well, also from the very beginning. Therefore, they are pure from the very beginning and no 'purification' or 'transformation' happens here at all. Instead, due to the realization of the true nature, the primordial awareness is seen in the affliction. Likewise, the primordial awareness is seen in the consciousness.

56. *Ratna* is Sanskrit for jewel or preciousness.

57. The Yogachara-madhyamaka philosophy (Shentong) ('empty of other' school) defines the absolute truth as primordial awareness free from mental projections and empty of anything other than itself.

58. 'Heart-essence of those gone to bliss' (Skt. *sugatagarbha*): *Sugata*, the one gone to bliss, is synonymous with 'Buddha', and *garbha* designates the heart-essence. Thus *sugatagarbha* designates the buddha-nature, or rather, as Rinpoche says here, the five kinds of primordial awareness.

59. The white and red aspects are the respective share of the parents that bring about the formation of the body. The father's semen (white) and the mother's egg (red, as in the association with menstrual blood) come together and cause the body to grow. Thereby the two aspects are pushed apart, to abide for as long as one lives as a white drop at the crown of one's head and as a red drop positioned below the navel. A detailed and clearly

comprehensible description of the development of the body may be found in Tenga Rinpoche's book on the six kinds of bardo: *Transition & Liberation*, pp. 15-19.

60. As for the dissolution of the elements and thoughts of mental afflictions, see also Tenga Rinpoche, ibid., pp. 44-50, "The Bardo of the Time of Death."

61. It is part of the bardo of the time of death, in which there is the greatest possibility for the supreme attainment, the attainment of buddhahood as dharmakaya at the time of death.

62. During his course on the bardo, August 1999, in the German retreat-center of Halscheid, I had the possibility to ask Rinpoche for further clarification on this point: The multiplication factor is five. This means that one is able to rest five times longer within the recognition of the true nature as one was able to do while alive. In addition, one 'day of mental stability' refers to the hours spent in uncontrived meditation. Precisely speaking, one hour of meditation while alive makes five so-called 'days of mental stability', in actuality these being five worldly hours.

63. A Buddha in his sambhogakaya aspect is adorned with eight kinds of jewel ornaments and five kinds of silk ornaments. The jewel ornaments are head ornaments, earrings, neck ornaments, bracelet, rings for the legs, short necklace, long necklace, and apron. The silk ornaments are crown-ribbon, long shawl, shirt, trousers, and belt.

64. By recognizing these bardo appearances to be the Buddhas, one can attain buddhahood as sambhogakaya in the bardo. A more detailed explanation of the appearance of the five Buddhas, and of the methods of training to recognize them, may be found in Tenga Rinpoche, ibid., pp. 51-93, "The Bardo of Dharmata."

65. These are birds of Indian Buddhist mythology—their lower parts are like those of birds, their upper ones like those of human beings.

66. Usually one speaks of fifty wrathful deities appearing in the bardo. When I asked Rinpoche how these fifty correspond to the fifty-one pure mental formations, he said it is only a matter of counting. There are precisely fifty wrathful deities. The Buddha Heruka, however, also appears in the form of Chemchok Heruka, which is why he is counted twice: this then makes fifty-one in all.

67. The Kangyur is a collection of the Buddha's discourses.

68. The thögal practice is a special meditation method unique to the great perfection (Dzogchen) tradition, through which one can cause the direct appearance of the Buddhas of the five buddha-families.

69. The bardo of becoming is extensively described in *Transition & Liberation*, pp. 92-100, and also in all the many translations of "The Tibetan Book of the Dead."

GLOSSARY

ka

kun 'gro lnga - five ever-present [mental events]

kun grtags kyi bdag - completely imputed self

kun rdzob rten brel gyi snang ba - relative appearances that are dependent on each other and connected one with another

kun gzhi rnam par shes pa - all-base consciousness (Skt. *alayavijñana*)

rkal pa - karmic good fortune

skyes nas myong gyur gyi las - karmic actions with the result experienced after rebirth

skyong - to keep, to apply

kha

khams - element

mkhas pa - [Buddhist] scholar

khyad chos thun mong ma yin pa - extraordinary qualities that are not common

khyad pa - particular detail

khrid yig - manual

mkhyen pa phun sum tshogs pa - excellent knowledge

'khor ba - samsara, cyclic existence, conditioned existence

'khrul pa - delusion

'khrul snang - delusion-based appearances

ga

go 'phang - level, state

go 'byed pa - openness, to provide space

dge ba - positive

dge ba bcu gcig - eleven virtuous [mental events]

dgongs pa - enlightened intention

rgyal ba gongs pa'i brgyud pa - knowledge transmission of the victorious ones

rgyal ba rigs lnga - lords of the five buddha-families

rgyas pa - increasing [enlightened activity]

rgyu thog nas lta ba - looking whilst the mind is moving

rgyu mthun gyi 'bras bu - result in accordance with the cause

rgyun du 'jog pa - continuous setting

sgo lnga'i shes pa - consciousnesses of the five gates, the five sense consciousnesses

sgrib pa - obscurations [of mental afflictions and those impeding knowledge]

sgrib la lung ma bstan - obscuring and neutral

brgyud kyi rgyu - indirect cause

nga

nga gces 'dzin - self-cherishing

nga la chags pa - attachment to an I

ngar 'dzin - conception of an I

ngar sems - idea of an I

ngo spros - pointed out

ngo 'phrod - to recognize

ngo bo - essence

ngo bo nyid kyi sku - essence-body (Skt. *svabhavikakaya*)

ngor - to/ from the perspective

ngos 'dzin - to recognize

dngos kyi rgyu - direct cause

dngos sgrub - extraordinary achievements (Skt. *siddhi*)

dngos po'i gnas gtang ga re yin pa - the exact mode of being of all phenomena

mngon shes - extrasensory perception

ca

ci yang med pa - blank nothingness

bcud - extract

lce'i rnam shes - tongue consciousness

lce'i dbang po - tongue faculty

cha

cha mnyam - balance
chos kyi sku - body of a Buddha's qualities (Skt. *dharmakaya*)
chos kyi dbyings - expanse of emptiness (Skt. *dharmadhatu*)
chos can - phenomena
chos nyid - true nature of phenomena (Skt. *dharmata*)

ja

ji snye par mkhyen pa'i ye shes - primordial awareness that knows
 the nature of reality to its full extent
ji lta bar mkhyen pa'i ye shes - primordial awareness that knows the
 nature of reality exactly as it is
'jug shes drug, 'jug pa'i rnam par shes pa tshogs drug - the six apprehending consciousnesses
'jog pa - setting [the mind]
rjes thob - post-meditational phase
rjes dpag lam du byed pa - using inference as the path

nya

nyams su blang ba - to put into practice
nyon sgrib - obscurations of mental afflictions
nyon mongs pa can gyi yid - klesha-mind, mind endowed with mental afflictions
nyon mongs pa'i sems byung - mental events of the mental afflictions
mnyam par bzhag pa - to rest in equipoise
mnyam bzhag - within meditation
nye pa'i nyon mongs - secondary afflictions

ta

ting nge dzin - meditative concentration (Skt. *samadhi*)
gti mugs - (mental) dullness
gtod pa - to concentrate, visualize
rten med la sems 'dzin pa - holding the mind without a basis
rtog bcas kyi shes pa - consciousness involving thoughts
rtog med kyi shes pa - thought-free consciousness
rtogs pa - realization
rtogs pa phun sum tshogs pa - excellent realization
stong nyid ma bu phrad pa - mother- and child-emptiness uniting
brtan pa'i rnam par shes pa - stable consciousness

tha

thar thug gi ye shes - ultimate primordial awareness
thibs pa - drowsiness
thugs la nus pa phun sum tshogs pa - excellent power of mind
thun mong - common
thun mong ma yin pa - extraordinary
mthong chos myong gyur gyi las - karmic actions with the result
   being experienced in this life

da

dam hri ge ba - rigid and inflexible
dwangs cha - clarity aspect
de ma thag tu - immediately
de ma thag yid - immediate mind
don spyi, don gyi spyi - mental image
don yod grub pa - Amoghasiddhi, the 'One Who Accomplishes What
   Is Meaningful'
dran pa - mindfulness
dran shes - alert mindfulness
gdon - spirits
bdag bskyed - self-visualization
bdag mchog dzin pa - to take the self to be the highest and the best
bdag med pa - non-existence of a self
bdag dzin - grasping at a self
bde skyid - happiness and joy
bde bar gzhegs pa'i snying po - heart-essence of those gone to bliss
   (Skt. *sugatagarbha*)
mdun bskyed - in-front visualization
sde snod gsum - three collections of the Buddha's talks (Skt. *tripitaka*)
sde tshan - category
ldangs ba - to emerge
du byed - mental formations
dul bya - those to be trained

na

nus pa - ability
gnas skabs kyi - temporary
gnas gyur - to transform
gnas thog nas lta ba - looking whilst the mind is resting
gnas tshul - way of being

gnas lugs - true nature

rna ba'i rnam shes - ear consciousness

rna ba'i dbang po - ear faculty

rnam pa - forms of expression, aspect, kinds

rnam par rtog pa - thoughts

rnam par snang mdzad - Vairochana, the 'One Who Completely Manifests'

rnam par smin pa'i kun gzhi - all-base of complete ripening

rnam par shes pa tshogs brgyad - the eight collections of consciousness

rnam smin gyi 'bras bu - completely ripened result

rnam shes - consciousness, aspect of consciousness

rnam shes tshogs drug - the six collections of consciousness: eye, ear, nose, tongue, body, and mind consciousness

rnam g.yeng - distraction

sna'i rnam shes - nose consciousness

sna'i dbang po - nose faculty

pa

spangs pa phun sum tshogs pa - excellent abandonment

spyod lam - ordinary behavior, everyday activities

sprul sku/ mchog gyi sprul sku - highest emanation body (Skt. *nirmanakaya*)

spros pa - mental projections

spros pa dang bral ba - freedom from mental projections

pha

phyin ci ma log pa - unadulterated

phrin las - enlightened activity [pacifying, increasing, empowering, and wrathful]

phag pa - noble one (Skt. *arya*)

'phags pa'i lam yan lag brgyad - eightfold path of the noble ones

ba

bag chags - karmic imprints

bag chags 'dzin pa'i kun gzhi - all-base that seizes karmic impressions

bying ba - dullness

brag po - wrathful

dbang - empowering

dbang rten - faculty basis
dbang du 'dus pa - to gain control over
dbang po sgo lnga - five sense faculties (Skt. *indriya*)
dbang po bye brag pa - specific faculties
dbyibs - shape
'ben po dul du grub pa - matter composed of atoms
'byung ba - element
'bras bu - result, fruition

ma

ma sgrib lung ma bstan - non-obscuring and neutral
ma rig pa - ignorance
mi bskyod pa - Akshobhya, the 'Unshakeable One'
mi dge ba - negative, non-virtuous
mi brtan pa'i rnam par shes pa - unstable consciousness
mig gi rnam shes - eye consciousness
mig gi dbang po - eye faculty
mos pa - steadfast conviction
myong bar ma nges pa'i las - karmic actions with uncertainty over
    the experience of a result
dmigs pa - to concentrate, to focus
dmigs bcas la sems 'dzin pa - holding the mind with a focus
dmigs med la sems 'dzin pa - holding the mind without any focus
rmugs pa - haziness
rmongs pa - infatuation

tsa

rtsa ba'i nyon mongs - root afflictions
rtsal - display, energy-potential
rtsal bton pa - to generate the energy-potential
rtse ba phun sum tshogs pa - excellent love
rtsol - to grant
gtso sems - principal mind
btsan thabs - intensive

tsha

tsha zhing sreg pa - hot and burning
mtshan nyid - defining characteristics
mtshon byed - symbolic attribute

dza

'dzin pa - grasping at, seizing

zha

zhag gyi nam drang - number of days
zhi ba - peaceful, pacifying [enlightened activity]
zhi gnas - calm abiding (Skt. *shamatha*)
gzhan 'gyur bzhi - four variable [mental events]
gzhan ngos nas - from the perspective of other beings

za

gzag bcas kyi dge ba - defiled virtue
gzugs dwangs ma - clear form
gzugs snyan - reflection

'a

'od dpag med - Amitabha, 'Infinite Light'

ya

yang zhing g.yo ba - light and moving
yid kyi rnam shes - mind consciousness
yul nges lnga - the five [mental events] with certainty over the object
yul drug - the six sense objects: forms, sounds, smells, tastes, physically tangibles, and phenomena
ye shes thob pa'i rgyu bzhi - four causes for attaining primordial awareness
ye shes gnas 'gyur pa'i rgyu bzhi - four causes for the transformation into primordial awareness
g.yo sgul - to surge up

ra

rang ngos nas - from one's own perspective
rang rtags - inherent indication
rang snang - self-appearances
rang dbang - independently
rang gzugs - self-expression
rang shugs - automatically
rags pa - coarse

rig 'dzin brda'i brgyud pa - symbol transmission of the awareness
  holders
rigs - potential
rin chen 'byung gnas - Ratnasambhava, 'Source of Preciousness'

la

lan grang gzhan la myong gyur gyi las - karmic actions with the result
  experienced after an uncertain number [of rebirths]
lung ma bstan - neutral
long spyod rdzogs pa'i sku - body of perfect enjoyment (Skt.
  sambhogakaya)
rlan zhing gsher ba - fluid and adhesive
bslan te 'jog pa - resetting [the mind]

sha

shes rab - highest understanding (Skt. *prajña*)
shes rab yum gyi rnam pa - female wisdom manifestation
shes bya'i sgrib pa - obscurations impeding knowledge
shes bzhin - alertness

sa

sangs rgyas chos kyi sku thob pa - attainment of a Buddha's quality
  body
sems gnas rim pa dgu - nine stages of mind coming to rest
sems byung - mental events
so so - specifically, individually
so so'i skye bo - ordinary person
sra zhing 'thas pa - solid and hard
srog lung rgyal po lta bu - royal life-force
gsal ba - clearly manifest
gsal snang - clear appearance
gsal cha - clarity aspect
gsal zhing rig pa - clear and cognizing
bsam gtan - mental stability
bsam gtan gyi zhag - one day of mental stability

ha

lhag mthong - deep insight (Skt. *vispashyana*)
lhan skyes kyi bdag - spontaneously present self
lhan cig tu - simultaneously

ENGLISH-TIBETAN

ability - *nus pa*
Akshobhya, the 'Unshakeable One' - *mi bskyod pa*
alert mindfulness - *dran shes*
alertness - *shes bzhin*
all-base that seizes karmic impressions - *bag chags 'dzin pa'i kun gzhi*
all-base of complete ripening - *rnam par smin pa'i kun gzhi*
all-base consciousness (Skt. *alayavijñana*) - *kun gzhi rnam par shes pa*
Amitabha, 'Infinite Light' - *'od dpag med*
Amoghasiddhi, the 'One Who Accomplishes What Is Meaningful'
    - *don yod grub pa*
attachment to an I - *nga la chags pa*
attainment of a Buddha's quality body - *sangs rgyas chos kyi sku
    thob pa*
automatically - *rang shugs*

balance - *cha mnyam*
blank nothingness - *mngon shes*
body of perfect enjoyment (Skt. *sambhogakaya*) - *long spyod rdzogs
    pa'i sku*
body of a Buddha's qualities (Skt. *dharmakaya*) - *chos kyi sku*
[Buddhist] scholar - *mkhas pa*

calm abiding (Skt. *shamatha*) - *zhi gnas*
category - *sde tshan*
clarity aspect - *gsal cha, dwangs cha*
clear and cognizing - *gsal zhing rig pa*
clear form - *gzugs dwangs ma*
clear appearance - *gsal snang*
clearly manifest - *gsal ba*
coarse - *rags pa*
common - *thun mong*
completely imputed self - *kun grtags kyi bdag*
completely ripened result - *rnam smin gyi 'bras bu*
to concentrate, to visualize - *gtod pa*
to concentrate, to focus - *dmigs pa*
conception of an I - *ngar 'dzin*

consciousness involving thoughts - *rtog bcas kyi shes pa*
consciousness, aspect of consciousness - *rnam shes*
consciousnesses of the five gates, the five sense consciousnesses -
    sgo lnga'i shes pa
continuous setting - *rgyun du 'jog pa*

deep insight (Skt. *vispashyana*) - *lhag mthong*
defiled virtue - *gzag bcas kyi dge ba*
defining characteristics - *mtshan nyid*
delusion - *'khrul pa*
delusion-based appearances - *'khrul snang*
direct cause - *dngos kyi rgyu*
display, energy-potential - *rtsal*
distraction - *rnam g.yeng*
drowsiness - *thibs pa*
dullness - *gti mugs, bying ba*

ear consciousness - *rna ba'i rnam shes*
ear faculty - *rna ba'i dbang po*
the eight collections of consciousness - *rnam par shes pa tshogs brgyad*
eightfold path of the noble ones - *'phags pa'i lam yan lag brgyad*
element - *khams, 'byung ba*
eleven virtuous [mental events] - *dge ba bcu gcig*
to emerge - *ldangs ba 'du byed*
empowering - *dbang*
enlightened activity [pacifying, increasing, empowering, and
    wrathful] - *phrin las*
enlightened intention - *dgongs pa*
essence - *ngo bo*
essence-body (Skt. *svabhavikakaya*) - *ngo bo nyid kyi sku*
the exact mode of being of all phenomena - *dngos po'i gnas gtang
    ga re yin pa*
excellent abandonment - *spangs pa phun sum tshogs pa*
excellent knowledge - *mkhyen pa phun sum tshogs pa*
excellent love - *rtse ba phun sum tshogs pa*
excellent realization - *rtogs pa phun sum tshogs pa*
excellent power of mind - *thugs la nus pa phun sum tshogs pa*
expanse of emptiness (Skt. *dharmadhatu*) - *chos kyi dbyings*
extract - *bcud*
extraordinary achievements (Skt. *siddhi*) - *dngos sgrub*

extraordinary qualities that are not common - *khyad chos thun mong
    ma yin pa*
extraordinary - *thun mong ma yin pa*
extrasensory perception - *mngon shes*
eye consciousness - *mig gi rnam shes*
eye faculty - *mig gi dbang po*

faculty basis - *dbang rten*
female wisdom manifestation - *shes rab yum gyi rnam pa*
five ever-present [mental events] - *kun 'gro lnga*
the five [mental events] with certainty over the object - *yul nges
    lnga*
five sense faculties (Skt. *indriya*) - *dbang po sgo lnga*
fluid and adhesive - *rlan zhing gsher ba*
forms of expression, aspect, kinds - *rnam pa*
four causes for attaining primordial awareness - *ye shes thob pa'i
    rgyu bzhi*
four causes for the transformation into primordial awareness - *ye
    shes gnas 'gyur pa'i rgyu bzhi*
four variable [mental events] - *gzhan 'gyur bzhi*
freedom from mental projections - *spros pa dang bral ba*
from one's own perspective - *rang ngos nas*
from the perspective of the other beings - *gzhan ngos nas*

to gain control over - *dbang du 'dus pa*
to generate the energy-potential - *rtsal bton pa*
to grant - *rtsol ba*
grasping at a self - *bdag 'dzin*
grasping at, seizing - *'dzin pa*

happiness and joy - *bde skyid*
haziness - *rmugs pa*
heart-essence of those gone to bliss (Skt. *sugatagarbha*) - *bde bar
    gzhegs pa'i snying po*
highest emanation body (Skt. *nirmanakaya*) - *sprul sku/ mchog gyi
    sprul sku*
highest understanding (Skt. *prajña*) - *shes rab*
holding the mind with a focus - *dmigs bcas la sems 'dzin pa*
holding the mind without a basis - *rten med la sems 'dzin pa*
holding the mind without any focus - *dmigs med la sems 'dzin pa*
hot and burning - *tsha zhing sreg pa*

idea of an I - *ngar sems*
ignorance - *ma rig pa*
immediately - *de ma thag tu*
immediate mind - *de ma thag yid*
increasing [enlightened activity] - *rgyas pa*
independently - *rang dbang*
indirect cause - *brgyud kyi rgyu*
infatuation - *rmongs pa*
in-front visualization - *mdun bskyed*
inherent indication - *rang rtags*
intensive - *btsan thabs*

karmic actions with the result being experienced in this life -
   mthong chos myong gyur gyi las
karmic actions with the result experienced after an uncertain number [of rebirths] - *lan grang gzhan la myong gyur gyi las*
karmic actions with the result experienced after rebirth - *skyes nas*
   myong gyur gyi las
karmic actions with uncertainty over the experience of a result -
   myong bar ma nges pa'i las
karmic good fortune - *rkal pa*
karmic imprints - *bag chags*
to keep, to apply - *skyong*
klesha-mind, mind endowed with mental afflictions - *nyon mongs*
   pa can gyi yid
knowledge transmission of the victorious ones - *rgyal ba gongs*
   pa'i brgyud pa

level, state - *go 'phang*
light and moving - *yang zhing g.yo ba*
looking whilst the mind is moving - *rgyu thog nas lta ba*
looking whilst the mind is resting - *gnas thog nas lta ba*
lords of the five buddha-families - *rgyal ba rigs lnga*

manual - *khrid yig*
matter composed of atoms - *'ben po dul du grub pa*
meditative concentration (Skt. *samadhi*) - *ting nge 'dzin*
mental events - *sems byung*
mental events of the mental afflictions - *nyon mongs pa'i sems byung*
mental image - *don spyi, don gyi spyi*
mental formations - *ldangs ba*

mental projections - *spros pa*
mental stability - *bsam gtan*
mind consciousness - *yid kyi rnam shes*
mindfulness - *dran pa*
mother- and child-emptiness uniting - *stong nyid ma bu phrad pa*

negative, non-virtuous - *mi dge ba*
neutral - *lung ma bstan*
nine stages of mind coming to rest - *sems gnas rim pa dgu*
noble one (Skt. *arya*) - *'phag pa*
non-existence of a self - *bdag med pa*
non-obscuring and neutral - *ma sgrib lung ma bstan*
nose consciousness - *sna'i rnam shes*
nose faculty - *sna'i dbang po*
number of days - *zhag gyi nam drang*

obscurations [of mental afflictions and those impeding knowledge]
    - *sgrib pa*
obscurations impeding knowledge - *shes bya'i sgrib pa*
obscurations of mental afflictions - *nyon sgrib*
obscuring and neutral - *sgrib la lung ma bstan*
one day of mental stability - *bsam gtan gyi zhag*
ordinary behavior, everyday activities - *spyod lam*
ordinary person - *so so'i skye bo*

particular detail - *khyad pa*
peaceful, pacifying [enlightened activity] - *zhi ba*
phenomena - *chos can*
pointed out - *ngo spros*
positive - *dge ba*
post-meditational phase - *rjes thob*
potential - *rigs*
primordial awareness that knows the nature of reality exactly as it is
    - *ji lta bar mkhyen pa'i ye shes*
primordial awareness that knows the nature of reality to its full
    extent - *ji snye par mkhyen pa'i ye shes*
principal mind - *gtso sems*
to provide space - *go 'byed pa*
to put into practice - *nyams su blang ba*

Ratnasambhava, 'Source of Preciousness'- *rin chen 'byung gnas*

realization - *rtogs pa*
to recognize - *ngos 'dzin, ngo 'phrod*
reflection - *gzugs snyan*
relative appearances that are dependent on each other and con-
    nected one with another - *kun rdzob rten brel gyi snang ba*
resetting [the mind] - *bslan te 'jog pa*
to rest in equipoise - *mnyam par bzhag pa*
result, fruition - *'bras bu*
result in accordance to the cause - *rgyu mthun gyi 'bras bu*
rigid and inflexible - *dam hri ge ba*
root afflictions - *rmongs pa*
royal life-force - *srog lung rgyal po lta bu*

samsara, cyclic existence, conditioned existence - *'khor ba*
secondary afflictions - *nye pa'i nyon mongs*
self-appearances - *rang snang*
self-cherishing - *nga gces 'dzin*
self-expression - *rang gzugs*
self-visualization - *bdag bskyed*
setting [the mind] - *'jog pa*
shape - *dbyibs*
simultaneously - *lhan cig tu*
the six apprehending consciousnesses - *'jug shes drug, 'jug pa'i rnam
    par shes pa tshogs drug*
the six collections of consciousness: eye, ear, nose, tongue, body, and
    mind consciousness - *rnam shes tshogs drug*
the six sense objects: forms, sounds, smells, tastes, physically tan-
    gibles, and phenomena - *yul drug*
solid and hard - *sra zhing 'thas pa*
specific faculties - *dbang po bye brag pa*
specifically, individually - *so so*
spirits - *gdon*
spontaneously present self - *lhan skyes kyi bdag*
stable consciousness - *brtan pa'i rnam par shes pa*
steadfast conviction - *mos pa*
to surge up - *g.yo sgul*
symbol transmission of the awareness holders - *rig 'dzin brda'i
    brgyud pa*
symbolic attribute - *mtshon byed*

to take the self to be the highest and the best - *bdag mchog 'dzin pa*
temporary - *gnas skabs kyi*
those to be trained - *'dul bya*
thought-free consciousness - *rtog med kyi shes pa*
thoughts - *rnam par rtog pa*
three collections of the Buddha's talks (Skt. *tripitaka*) - *sde snod gsum*
to/ from the perspective - *ngor*
tongue consciousness - *lce'i rnam shes*
tongue faculty - *lce'i dbang po*
to transform - *gnas gyur*
true nature - *gnas lugs*
true nature of phenomena (Skt. *dharmata*) - *chos nyid*

ultimate primordial awareness - *thar thug gi ye shes*
unadulterated - *phyin ci ma log pa*
unstable consciousness - *mi brtan pa'i rnam par shes pa*
using inference as the path - *rjes dpag lam du byed pa*

Vairochana, the 'One Who Completely Manifests' - *rnam par snang mdzad*

way of being - *gnas tshul*
within meditation - *mnyam bzhag*
wrathful - *brag po*

LITERATURE

Geshe Rabten. *The Mind and Its Functions*. Trans. Stephen Batchelor. Le Mont-Pèlerin: Editions Rabten Choeling, 1992.

Guenther, Herbert V. and Leslie S. Kawamura. *Mind in Buddhist Psychology*. Berkeley: Dharma Publishing, 1975.

Jamgön Kongtrul Lodrö Thayé. *rNam shes ye shes 'byed pa'i grel pa rang byung dgongs rgyan* (Ornament of Rangjung Dorje's Intention in His Commentary that Distinguishes between Consciousness and Primordial Awareness). Sikkim: Karma Shri Nalanda Institute, 1990.

Jamgön Kongtrul Lodrö Thayé. *Shes bya kun khyab mdzod* (The Treasury of Knowledge). China: Mi rigs dpe skrun khang, 1982.

Jamgön Kongtrul Lodrö Thayé's "Treasury of Knowledge", Chapter Eight, Part One: "The Stages of Meditation of Shamatha and Vipashyana". Translated by Kiki Ekselius and Chryssoula Zerbini. Montignac, France: Dhagpo Kagyu Ling, 1985.

Lati Rinbochay. *Mind in Tibetan Buddhism*. Trans. Elizabeth Napper. Ithaca, New York: Snow Lion Publications, 1986.

Mipham Rinpoche. *Gateway to Knowledge*, Vol. 1. Trans. Erik Pema Kunsang. Boudhanath, Hong Kong and Esby: Rangjung Yeshe Publications, 1997.

Nyingma Education Series. *Ways of Enlightenment*, based on Mipham-rgya-mtsho's *mKhas 'jug*. Berkeley: Dharma Publishing, 1993.

Rangjung Dorje, Karmapa. *rNam shes ye shes byed pa'i bstan bcos* (The Treatise that Distinguishes between Consciousness and

Primordial Awareness). Sikkim: Karma Shri Nalanda Institute, 1990.

Rangjung Dorje, Karmapa. *Von der Klarheit des Geistes.* Trans. Tina and Alex Draszczyk. Vienna: Marpa Verlag, 1995.

Sangye Gyamtso. *Tibetan Medical Paintings, Illustrations to the Blue Beryl.* New York: Harry N. Abrams, 1992.

Tenga Rinpoche. *Transition & Liberation.* Trans. Susanne Schefczyk. Osterby: Khampa Buchverlag, 1999.

Tsültrim Gyamtso Rinpotsche. *Die Darstellung der Klassifikation der Bewußtseinszustände, genannt "Der Wesenskern des Ozeans der Logiktexte,"* Trans. Karl Brunnhölzl. Hamburg: Marpa Translation Committee, 1995.

Tsultrim Gyamtso Rinpoche, Khenpo and Shenpen Hookham. *Progressive Stages of Meditation on Emptiness.* Oxford: Longchen Foundation, 1986.